John and Betty
Stam

MEN OF FAITH SERIES

Borden of Yale
C. S. Lewis
Charles Finney
Charles Spurgeon
George Muller
Hudson Taylor
Jonathan Goforth
John Hyde
John Wesley
Samuel Morris
William Carey

John and Betty Stam

WOMEN OF FAITH SERIES

Florence Nightingale
Gladys Aylward
Isobel Kuhn
Mary Slessor

John and Betty
Stam

Kathleen White

BETHANY HOUSE PUBLISHERS
MINNEAPOLIS, MINNESOTA 55438
A Division of Bethany Fellowship, Inc.

John and Betty Stam
Kathleen White

Library of Congress Catalog Card Number 89-82133

ISBN 1-55661-124-2

First published by Marshall Morgan and Scott
Publications Ltd

Published by Bethany House Publishers
A Ministry of Bethany Fellowship, Inc.
6820 Auto Club Road, Minneapolis, Minnesota 55438

Printed in the United States of America

Contents

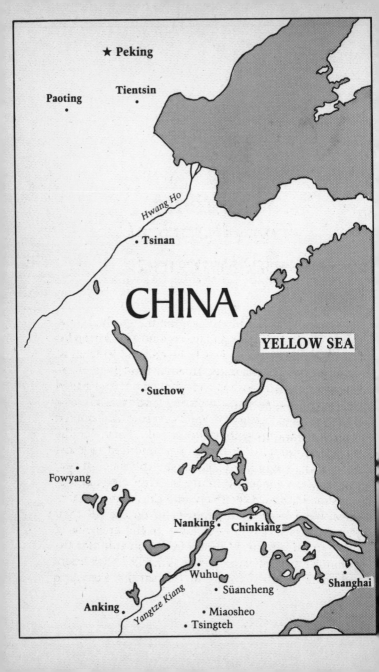

1

The Historical Background

A clump of tall pine trees dominated the scene. Their dark green foliage created a backdrop for the tragedy that was to be enacted in front of them. In the distance, the irregular roof lines of the Chinese city of Miaosheo were picked out and gilded by the rays of the early morning sunshine. On one side a group of unkempt Communist soldiers shouted roughly at the assembled townsfolk. They, for the most part peasants or tradesmen, huddled together in silence, stunned by the events of the last few hours. Many longed to refute the ridiculous allegations made against the two white Christian missionaries, but lacked the willpower to do so. All their moral courage had drained away in the presence of these ruthless men. Within a few short minutes the ground at the foot of the trees was marked with bright red pools, mute witness to the savage execution which had just taken place. If, as is so often claimed, the blood of martyrs is the seed of the Church, another sowing had just been carried out which would produce a worldwide harvest.

Yet the land of China was no stranger to blood-letting. Blood had stained the pages of its history on innumerable occasions. China's people had endured centuries of savage wars, internal rebellions and massacres, although the news took a long time to filter through to the world outside which was also used to periods of war and violence among the more Western nations.

Equally, too, China had enjoyed eras of peace and prosperity, producing men of great intellectual powers and craftsmen whose fertile minds and deft fingers created objects of rare beauty—like pictures and lengths of delicate spun silk, most sought after throughout the world. At a later date they were also responsible for useful inventions like movable type.

From earliest times, as in other countries, their civilization had grown up along the shores of a river. For them it was the Hwang-Ho or Yellow River in North China, about two hundred miles south of the modern capital city of Peking, which provided the base for their earliest settlement. This same river that yielded rich alluvial soil for these early farmers to sow their crops often brought death and destruction in its wake, when the swirling waters caused by torrential floods swept away all buildings and living creatures in its path. This constant battle with the elements produced outstanding men who responded to the challenge by pitting their wits against this lethal foe. By their ingenuity they devised means of escape for the people and eventually set up irrigation schemes to drain away the surplus water and use it to benefit the growing crops.

Over the centuries, several dynasties evolved with emperors of varying importance. Even a couple of thousand years before Christ was born, primitive forms of writing were worked out. From early times, quite sophisticated metalwork was produced. The wheel, with all its consequent application to both domestic and military vehicles, was invented. Chinese workers were the first to discover a process by which raw silk from cocoons could be spun and then woven into beautiful lengths of delicate material. It was this product, more than any other, that appeared so desirable to other nations.

Eagerly traders tried to find out the secret of this manufacturing, but the Chinese managed to withhold it from them. So merchants from the West were compelled to set off on long, tortuous journeys to obtain this exotic fabric. Communications were slow and dangerous and involved treks of thousands of miles for the slow-moving caravans. It was this factor of isolation that not only governed China's dealings with Western nations, but also influenced the West's conception of the Chinese and their unique way of life. Distance fostered ignorance because so few Europeans were prepared to risk their lives to set out on such a monumental trip to find out the truth for themselves about those yellow-skinned people. Consequently, not a great deal was known about Chinese people and their customs, and many rumors and far-fetched travelers' tales abounded.

Yet far from being a nation of ignorant peasants,

Chinese society evolved in quite a sophisticated way. True, slaves did exist, many of them being taken as prisoners-of-war from the marauding tribes who invaded from the north from time to time. But the middle and upper classes enjoyed a high standard of living in comfortable, well-appointed townhouses.

It was not only the sheer length of the journey that prevented traders and explorers from finding out more about this mighty nation that was developing. It was also the great natural barriers that abounded and cut China off from outside influences. The huge peaks of the Himalayan range separated China from the country of India. To the north and west lay vast tracts of desert and a sea voyage involved a long detour around the peninsula of Malaya before the coast of China could be reached.

In addition, a formidable feat of engineering was constructed between the years of 218–204 B.C. This was known as the Great Wall of China, of which a considerable portion is still in existence today. It stretched for over fourteen hundred miles, and, like Britain's own Antonine and Hadrian Walls, possessed turrets at regular intervals which were useful as outposts for sentries and border guards. It meant that a vast area of the country could be maintained, keeping a watch on strangers who lived outside the protection of the walls. The Emperor responsible for this, Huang-Ti, also built roads and canals. With better means of communication, the country, although huge, was more united.

Centuries later, ambitious emperors set out to conquer other nations lying on the Chinese borders. But, in spite of infiltration into these lands, the

Chinese people on the whole did not integrate with other people more than was absolutely necessary for relatively local conquest or trade. They still remained an enigma to curious Westerners, and their civilization was largely unaffected by the rest of the world.

Some of these same factors were probably responsible for the delay in the arrival of the Christian message to these people. Although the Gospel had begun to spread around the shores of the Mediterranean Sea by the end of the first century A.D., and had been carried into the hinterland by Roman military and civil converts, even reaching the remote island of Britain, as archaeological and written evidence conclusively proves, the main thrust and emphasis of Christianity was westward from the Holy Land. It took much longer to make any appreciable impact on the Orient.

A dramatic breach of the Great Wall in three places by Mongolian hordes under Genghis Khan at the beginning of the thirteenth century put a stop to some of China's former policy of isolation. Mongols also broke through as far as Hungary and Poland, so enabling the rest of the world to appreciate China's wealth, culture and almost unlimited resources. Trade routes, which up to that time had been extremely hazardous, opened up more freely and offered new opportunities to Western merchants and traders.

It was toward the end of this century that Marco Polo's incredible adventures took place, bringing further revelations about the inscrutable Chinese, whose way of life differed so greatly from Polo's childhood in Venice. At first, it was his father and uncle who set off on a trading mission to Russia. Cut off by war, they were compelled to travel by a different route. After nine years' absence, the Venetians had given them up for lost, but one day they turned up again, weather-beaten, sun-tanned, and with a breathtaking story. They had been invited to visit the court of Kublai Khan in his capital of Peking. Fascinated to meet Westerners for the first time, the emperor had been reluctant to let them return.

They carried with them, however, a letter from him to no less a personage than the Pope, asking him to send one hundred learned monks to convert the Mongols to Christianity. What a golden opportunity for the Church! It took some time to reassemble the personnel for the new expedition, but surprisingly, when it was complete, only two Dominican monks joined the party. Why Christians did not rush to meet this missionary challenge has never been satisfactorily explained. The appeal met with apathy and even the two that set out turned back rather faintheartedly at the first sign of danger. How different might have been the history of China if the full complement had volunteered to accompany the Polos, with corresponding crusading zeal!

Marco, the youngest member of the party, travelled the whole expedition and remained away from his homeland a full twenty-four years. On his return, he and his father and uncle again had some difficulty convincing the Venetians who they were. But one further adventure awaited Marco—while serving as an officer on board a galleon in a war with Genoa, he was taken prisoner. The scribe with whom he shared a cell was fascinated by Marco's tales of travel, and insisted on writing it all down—without which posterity may never have had the full story.

It is certainly curious to note that two middle-aged Italians could whet Kublai Khan's appetite for Christianity, a religion completely foreign to the Chinese philosophy.

After Kublai Khan's death, China once more closed her doors to outsiders and tried to run her own affairs without interference. Over the centuries, this created a kind of time warp where development in science, industry, agriculture and politics hardly made any progress. Eventually, in the middle of the nineteenth century, the Manchu emperor appealed to Western European powers. This of course paved the way for France and Britain to establish trading posts. It was then that Christian missionaries were admitted again.

Then in 1900, Chinese nationals turned against foreigners living in their trading posts and cities. The Boxer Rebellion broke out and many people were cruelly massacred. These riots were finally suppressed, but not without great loss of life—which left Westerners with an obvious feeling of insecurity. And although there was some semblance of peace, foreigners knew well what savagery the Chinese were capable of when their passions were roused.

This rebellion was not merely aimed at Christians from missionary societies, although many did suffer through that period. Chinese peasants greatly resented any Westerners who came to settle in their country, particularly traders who made fortunes, as they thought, at their expense. Many misunderstandings also arose through lack of communication—the language being difficult to learn with so many completely foreign characters. And because they had largely been closed off from the outside world for so long, the Chinese found foreign ways of life strange and incomprehensible.

Steeped as the Chinese were in the sayings of Confucius and other ancient scholars, and accustomed to the practices in the Buddhist temples, it was difficult for Europeans to make inroads into their philosophy of life. Preaching Christianity to impoverished, fearsome savages proved almost easier for missionaries than trying to convert Chinese with their long history of culture and civilization behind them. Missionaries who volunteered for service in China had to be courageous, extremely hardworking, and possess the magic quality of "stick-to-it-tiveness." Cut off from home by a perilous sea voyage of several weary months, they risked not only their own lives, but that of their children, in a mainly hostile environment and difficult climate. Fortunately, some real heroes of faith were not deterred.

2

The Birth of the China Inland Mission

So when John Stam and Elisabeth Alden Scott, at the end of their training at Moody Bible Institute, decided independently of each other to volunteer for service in China with the China Inland Mission, it was no casual impulse that led them to take that step. Conditions in the country in June 1930 were at best threatening—hardly conducive to persuade a young couple to leave the affluent and stable United States of America to risk an uncertain future in a faraway foreign land. Communist armies had overrun the larger part of the province of Kiangsi, and it was by no means a peaceable takeover. Brutal killings abounded—three members of the China Inland Mission had already lost their lives, and a married couple were still in captivity, held by the rebel troops.

So, one might ask, why did the China Inland Mission appeal particularly to these young people? What was so special about it that attracted people from so many parts of the world? The mission was not organized until the latter half of the nineteenth century, but its origins lay in the 1700's. About eighty-five years before its organization, the conversion of a simple countryman in Yorkshire had a profound effect upon missionary enterprise in England. No one could have foretold it at the time, but by a remarkable chain of events it led to the largest single factor in converting many thousands of Chinese to Christ—another mighty oak sprung from a tiny acorn.

James Taylor of Royston, Yorkshire, on his wedding day—February 1, 1776, was suddenly and inexplicably arrested in his thoughts during his hectic preparations to make his cottage sparkling clean to receive his young bride. Perhaps the responsibility of setting up a household of his own for the first time weighed upon him, for normally he was known to be a singer and extremely fond of dancing. But as he worked away at his chores before setting out for church, the words kept coming to his mind: "As for me and my house we will serve the Lord."

Could that truly be said of him and his bride Betty? The great John Wesley himself had come into the district about five years previously, urging people to do just that—but James as a young lad had not heeded the appeal. The godly lifestyle of many of the Methodist families scattered around in the villages had not attracted him in the effervescence of youth, but now the thoughts of all that marriage entailed, and the possibility of bringing up children himself, brought him to his knees. A solemn transaction was forged in that hour between the young stonemason and his Creator, before he rose to his feet, newly conscious of his many duties on that momentous day.

Quickly covering the two miles on foot between his humble cottage and the parish church at Royston, James arrived breathless, but with great joy in his heart—in time to allay the fears of those who were anxiously waiting for the marriage ceremony to begin.

His wife Betty no doubt became his first convert. Considerably dismayed at first by the new priorities in her husband's life, she resisted his attempts to preach to her the Gospel. She very much resented family prayers and Bible reading as part of their daily routine, making it difficult for him to carry them out. But James quietly yet firmly persisted, and it was not long before she too had been won over to his way of thinking.

Ten years later, John Wesley visited the Barnsley area again, setting his seal on the work already carried out by his enthusiastic converts. In his journal he wrote: "Friday, June 30, 1786: I turned aside to Barnsley, formerly famous for all manner of wickedness. They were ready to tear any Methodist preacher to pieces. Now, not a dog wagged its tongue. I preached near the Market Place to a very large congregation, and I believe the truth sank into many hearts. They seemed to drink in every word."

The torch of the testimony of Jesus Christ's followers was handed down in unbroken succession in the Taylor family. In 1832, James' great-grandson was born—James Hudson Taylor, combining the names of both parents. This child grew to become the founder of the China Inland Mission. At age fourteen, with youthful sincerity, he gave his heart to God—experiencing a few spiritual ups and downs before becoming thoroughly committed to the idea of serving God overseas. Writing to his sister, while still a teenager, he confessed: "I have a stronger desire than ever to go to China. That land is ever in my thoughts. Think of it—three hundred and sixty million souls, without God or hope in the world! Think of more than twelve million of our fellowmen dying every year without any consolation of the Gospel—and scarcely anyone cares about it."

After many years of tedious study and enormous self-sacrifice in organizing his meager financial resources, James Hudson Taylor finally set sail for China in 1854. Circumstances proved far from favorable, when he arrived after a perilous voyage of five months. Shanghai was still in the grip of war, accommodations were almost unobtainable, and food was scarce and costly. What medical training he had was immediately called into action to attend the wounded in street fighting right outside his window.

At first Taylor went out under the auspices of the Chinese Evangelization Society, but association with them became difficult through the next few years. Wearing Chinese national costume, and gradually relying solely on the Lord for financial support, Hudson Taylor knew both the triumph of winning Chinese souls for Christ and the exhaustion of working superhuman hours in impossible circumstances. But his resolution never wavered in spite of all the obstacles and setbacks.

Toward the end of his first term of service in

China, Hudson Taylor was preaching as usual one evening, when a prosperous cotton merchant—Mr. Nee—passed the open door and was attracted by the sight of a young foreigner in national dress reading from sacred books. As an ex-Buddhist leader, Mr. Nee had long been in pursuit of the truth without any conviction in his heart that he had found "the way." Listening to Hudson Taylor's almost perfect enunciation in the Ningpo dialect, he first became intrigued. As the meeting progressed, he became convicted of sin and convinced he had at last discovered the answer to life's problems after years of searching.

Rising to his feet, he addressed the congregation in simple terms. All were struck by his directness: "I have long sought the Truth, but never found it. I have traveled far and near, but never discovered it. I have found no rest in Confucianism, Buddhism, or Taoism. But I have found rest in what we have heard tonight. Henceforth, I am a believer in Jesus!"

If anything could set the seal on Hudson Taylor's mission it was that straightforward declaration. No wonder the seed planted in his heart grew at a phenomenal rate, and it was not long before Mr. Nee himself began to lead others to Christ through his personal testimony.

Yet, it was this very man who also soon posed a personal challenge to Mr. Taylor in a particular conversation with him:

"How long have you had the Gospel in your country?"

"Some hundreds of years," came the reply.

"What! Hundreds of years? My father sought the Truth," he continued sadly, "and died without finding it. Why didn't you come sooner?"

Hudson Taylor never forgot this incident. Many times it was his only incentive—when conditions were tough and his frail human body weary—to spur him on to even greater efforts in pursuit of his goal.

After six action-packed years in China revising the Ningpo Testament, and five testing years in the East End of London resuming his medical studies, Hudson Taylor set out once more with his wife and four young children, together with a party of sixteen missionaries—with a vision to evangelize the whole of inland China. Unable to gain support for this objective from any of the established mission societies involved in that part of the world, he had no other option but to organize the China Inland Mission on his own initiative. Convinced that God had called him for this purpose, he reluctantly cut his former ties and stepped out in faith.

Although encouragement soon came in the form of new converts, there were plenty of entries on the debit side of the ledger. In writing to an English friend, Mrs. Taylor made the morose comment, "Perhaps the Lord sees that we need sorrows to keep us from being inflated over the rich blessings He is bestowing on our work." Ironically, the first fresh sorrow she was soon called upon to face, after penning that letter, was the death of their only daughter Grace, just eight years old. Later their five-year-old son succumbed to a chronic health problem, dying while his parents were making arrangements for him to travel to England with their other children, in the care of Hudson Taylor's devoted secretary.

Finally, Mrs Taylor's own life ebbed away after

giving birth to a son who survived but a short while. She lived just long enough to make arrangements for the infant's funeral, and to receive the news with gratitude that the other children had safely reached England and been given a warm and loving welcome by Mission staff and relatives there.

Even as Hudson Taylor knelt by her bed and committed her weary body to the Lord's safekeeping, with almost the same breath he solemnly rededicated himself to the Lord's service. Days and months of ill health and loneliness followed. Almost the first unenviable task he had to face was writing a letter to his poor, homesick children just newly arrived in England, that their mother had departed this life.

Later, Taylor became acquainted with Miss Faulding, the leader of the women's work in Hangchow, and she became his second wife—selflessly devoting herself to looking after, not only the family, but the whole Mission personnel. A familiar pattern continued—joy in new ground covered, new converts won for Christ, God's faithfulness in providing for their needs, and a steady influx of recruits to join the Mission; but sorrow too, in the unbelievable hardships. These included partial paralysis for Hudson Taylor at one point, and the brutal massacre of refugees in the Mission stations during the fierce Boxer Rebellion in 1900. Understandably could Taylor write at one stage: "Flesh and heart often fail; let them fail! He faileth not. Pray, very much, pray constantly, for Satan rages against us."

Even after his first wife's death, Hudson Taylor remained director of C.I.M. for another thirty fruitful years. With his tremendous wealth of firsthand experience, he could identify with any problem—spiritual or physical—that members of his staff were called upon to undergo. The caliber of China Inland Mission workers was that of fully-tempered fine steel. After Taylor's death in June 1905, the tradition of strong leadership and commitment lingered on in subsequent directors.

It is no wonder then that it was to the China Inland Mission that John and Betty Stam felt an attraction when they received a clear call to work in China.

3

John Stam

John's father, Peter Stam, had arrived in the United States of America from Holland in the early years of the twentieth century. Like so many others from Europe, he set out to find, if not fame, a fortune for himself in a new country that offered exciting opportunities to its would-be citizens. What he had no idea of seeking, however, became his soon after stepping on those shores, and it grew to be a far greater treasure than any of the goals he had originally set for himself in his youthful ambition.

Anxious to learn English, he began to study industriously. A keen Christian woman, seeing his need, presented him with a New Testament containing passages printed in both Dutch and English. She knew it would be of help to him, and prayed he might be affected by it. At the beginning, language was a priority, but after awhile the truth of what he was reading began to permeate his consciousness. For the first time in his life, Peter was aware of how God viewed him. He shared with her, "The book told me that I was a sinner . . . I tried not to believe it; but as I read on I had to be honest with myself, and confess that I was indeed a sinner. But the book also told me that God loved me." Here Peter quoted the universally known text of John 3:16: " '. . . whosoever believeth in Him should not perish [that meant me, too] but have everlasting life.' Then and there, I took up the offer, surrendered my life to Him who died for me, and began by His grace to live for others."

The last phrase of Peter's testimony was no idle statement. Convinced that a mere verbal profession was not enough, he set about finding underprivileged members of the community in need of love and kindness. The example of Christ who openly stated, "I am among you as one who serves" (Luke 22:27b), spurred him on. Visiting the sick in hospitals and the inmates in jails, he also found time for the elderly who lived in homes for the aged. But his vision was even larger than that. Peter did not confine his efforts to those living in institutions, but took an interest in anyone genuinely in need who sought his assistance.

A builder by trade, he developed his business to include a lumber yard and an insurance office. Peter was well known for his integrity; people soon found out that his standards of workmanship were always reliable, and his business flourished. He was fortunate enough to find for a wife someone who shared his nationality and his faith. He built their home himself, and although nothing elaborate was planned, he built a simple frame house which stood in an elevated position on Temple Hill, in Paterson, New Jersey. It had a distinguishing feature, a dome above the attic, which gave visitors a panoramic view of the whole city and the countryside beyond.

To Peter and his wife were born, in course of time, six sons and three daughters—one of them died in infancy. To some, their upbringing might seem rather restricted and prescribed, compared to youngsters growing up in the 1980's, but it was fairly characteristic of a Christian family at the beginning of the century, and in fact, a great deal of love was mixed with the discipline. They all attended the Christian Grammar School. Grace at meals, followed by Bible reading was accepted as part of everyday life. But their interests were not merely one-sided. A love of books was encouraged at an early age, and their interest in music was fostered by a family orchestra which gave them endless fun. Although adamant that they should not take part in certain "worldly pleasures" such as theater-going or dancing, Peter always took care to substitute special outings and activities. On the whole, the children accepted this regime even if they envied some of their school friends.

John, the seventh child and fifth son, was of a more independent nature than his brothers and sisters. His conversion was far from early and automatic. His father had started up a Mission, known as the Star of Hope, in an abandoned stable. Undeterred by its filthy condition, Peter was able to use his building skills to transform the stable into a large hall with a seating capacity of six hundred, as well as other rooms which were required for various social activities. Naturally, the family supported the work and became involved in the program, but John was not really touched by the gospel messages he heard there until, as a youth of fifteen, he became affected by the preaching of a blind evangelist.

Again his independent streak revealed itself, when he refused to enter higher education, although his father had offered to pay for it. A course at a small business college appealed to him more, and his father wisely let him follow his own bent. It was actually in a classroom at this school that he became a Christian in the early part of 1922. This radically changed his outlook, and although still conscientious and anxious to please, he sorted out his priorities so that ambition and success were no longer his first motivation.

Writing about John's life does present some difficulty, as so little source material is available. *Nihil nisi mortuisbonum*—nothing but good about the dead—is not an option a biographer chooses who wants to write honestly about his subject. Because of the nature of his death, one might be tempted to cast him as a saintly character out of touch with the world. But this would be far from the truth. An independence of spirit enabled John to assess everything on its own merit, such as not following blindly in the family traditions until he was thoroughly convinced that they were right for him. It would have been easier to please the family by becoming a Christian earlier in his life, and perhaps by spending a few more years in further study, yet John was never one to choose the easy way out, or to base his actions only on what others may think of him. This ability to face up to hard choices stood him in good stead later on in his life.

Certainly to volunteer for service in China

showed great courage and determination. The effort he put into learning the difficult Chinese language, with all its myriad foreign characters, also proved his capability for academic study when it was essential for the next stage in his life. He could always seem to rise to any occasion when required.

A more extroverted person, with John's background, might have thrown himself wholeheartedly into open-air preaching and campaign work. John, on the contrary, felt very shy and self-conscious at the mere thought of it—so much so, that as a teenager he made a point of walking in a wide detour to avoid any speaking or singing group out in the streets. It was a thoroughly natural reaction for a young person, but although he had given himself the breathing-space he thought he needed, he wasn't altogether happy with the situation. He had no peace of mind.

One day he asked his father with concern, "Why aren't the teams out preaching? It's summertime now, and they've usually started by this time. What's happened?"

Unknowingly, he had dug a trap for himself. "It's your business to make a start, John," replied his father cheerfully, leaving the matter to his son's conscience.

With fear and trembling, John began in a faltering way. The more experience he gained, the more confidently he tackled the matter, until he and his younger brother Neal found themselves out on the streets nearly every summer evening. Gone was his dread of being jeered at by school friends. Ridicule no longer troubled him.

It seemed as though this step had unlocked a new

facet of his personality. Reading a wide range of books gave him a great deal of intellectual pleasure and mental stimulation. Instead of appearing shy and introverted, he developed a lively interest in other people.

Many and varied were the faces of different nationalities that he scrutinized on his long jaunts through the contrasting quarters of New York City. Sometimes he strode along the great shopping boulevards with their opulent and scintillating window displays. At other times he walked through the seamier districts of the great city viewing for himself the crowded living conditions, and the squalor and deprivation endured in Chinatown and the black ghettos. In those days, airplanes were a rarity flown largely by pioneer aviators, anxious to break records or conquer hitherto unexplored routes. Sea-travel still remained the most usual method of traveling from one continent to another. John's office windows looked out over these international freighters and ocean liners. Perhaps they whet his appetite for journeying to foreign parts.

Actually, it was a combination of influences that made John Stam arrive at the momentous decision to abandon his secular career for the prospect of fulltime Christian work. His employers were reluctant to lose him, but once his mind was made up, nothing would change it. Wisely, he spent several months assisting at the Star of Hope Mission that his father had launched. He realized that he needed more experience than he had been able to gain up to that point, working evenings and weekends, before he was ready for a wider range of service.

The Moody Bible Institute of Chicago wa: lege he chose to further prepare himself. Ob Bible study and missionary training loomed large on his program of study. Yet his further motive was a deeper grounding in the faith and a desire to experience firsthand God's faithfulness in dealing with his servants. From his comfortable, secure home background, life had been relatively easy. His parents thoroughly approved of his involvement in Christian work, and after earning a salary for a few years, he was beginning to save something toward his future. It looked as though financial security was within reach.

For children brought up in a Christian home, it is often too easy to take on a second-hand faith, to have a second-hand experience of God's love and salvation. But John set high standards for himself—it had to be all or nothing. He longed to prove for himself the promises and faithfulness of God, and in so doing, enjoy a closer relationship with the Lord.

As a businessman, he was practical enough to realize that there might arise times when his financial resources could prove inadequate, or even be nonexistent. Would God be equal to occasions such as these? In theory, he would automatically answer in the affirmative, but he wanted to place himself in situations where God could become increasingly real to him. As long as he relied on his savings, he wasn't trusting God completely.

John's family and friends assumed that once his money was exhausted, he would confide in them for his needs. But, this was a course he had definitely decided not to follow. Hopefully, he would find a variety of jobs in Chicago which would help him pay for college tuition, books, and his room and board. "Whatever difficulties come my way, I'll tell God about them, and God alone," he told himself.

Even coming from a relatively large family, to be plunged into the maelstrom of one thousand students at Moody Institute must have seemed a severe "culture shock." Yet, in spite of the numbers, order was created out of what could have been chaos. One of his brothers who paid him a visit wryly commented, "There has to be order, with such a crowd!' A strict timetable was adhered to, and all the students shared in the preparation and clean-up of meals. Generally, the varied personalities and nationalities blended well, with hymn-singing reverberating all over the work rooms, even if it wasn't completely harmonious!

4

At Moody Bible Institute

*E*lecting to study at the Moody Bible Institute
was definitely not a soft option. Not being
blessed with rich endowments, the buildings
at the Institute were in need of remodeling and re-
decorating, and resources were not plentiful.

The missionary course of study that John chose
the first year proved challenging and demanding
with quite a strong emphasis on practical subjects.
John changed to the general course the following
year, and applied himself well to his studies, gaining
the reputation of an outstanding and unusual Christian student. Although a slow developer, he soon impressed his professors with his academic approach
to his work. It seemed as though he was at last coming
alive in three dimensions—body, soul and spirit. "He
was well-balanced and energetic, possessing a good
judgment and considerable initiative. In his practical
Christian work assignments, he proved to be a good
speaker and an exceptionally good group leader,"
read the secretary's report.

People openly expressed the opinion that one day John would make his mark on the world—quite a prophetic utterance, as it turned out. But no one at that stage could possibly have foretold what the future held for him, or what blueprint God had created for his life. All that lay ahead. Fortunately, John remained completely unaware of the comments being made about him. He found he could cope with the studies satisfactorily, but many other responsibilities crowded in upon him, such as special meetings for prayer and committee meetings. Essential as they might be to a student, they occupied much of his time, so that his own devotional times with the Lord became increasingly difficult to fit in.

John solved the problem by rising at five every morning, which meant a very long, concentrated day. It paid dividends, however, in that John became an example and encouragement to others around him. He had no illusions about himself, however, nor any wish to boast. "My only trouble is myself," he wrote to one of his brothers. He longed to rise above his own shortcomings and be a partaker of the victorious Christian life.

No wonder the apostle Paul compared the young Christian to a soldier and an athlete. There is always the need to strive, to compete, and above all to fight the good fight. A recurring problem for John was his financial supply. Having chosen not to make his needs known, there were times when his limited resources were really stretched. In writing to his missionary brother in the Belgian Congo, he stated, "The Lord has wonderfully taken care of me all through my stay here at Moody. The classroom studies are a blessing, but I think I've learned even more outside of classes."

Unsolicited gifts, however small, were gratefully accepted and never forgotten. He did not, however, rely totally on gifts to support himself. Being of a practical nature, John waited on tables three times a day in the college cafeteria, where nearly a thousand students took their meals. His efficiency did not go unnoticed, and eventually he was made supervisor of both the dining area and the kitchen. The financial reward was far from equal to the effort involved, but it made a welcome addition to his weekly income. John always rejoiced in spite of his stringent budget. He had proved to himself that God was more than equal to his needs.

Miracles, however insignificant to others, burned themselves on his memory. He loved to share how God provided for him—like the time when he found a five-dollar bill on the street, enabling him to purchase some warm shirts and thick socks to equip him for a previously dreaded long, cold journey home in a fellow student's car. "Every time I pull these socks on these cold nights, they preach a sermon to me on the Lord's wonderful power to provide, whatever my needs may be," he wrote a friend.

Five dollars may not seem like a great amount of money, but an even smaller sum—just an extra nickel found in a telephone slot—made it possible for him to make an important call, and increased his awareness of God watching over him.

Fortunately for us all, friends and family of John Stam treasured and preserved many of his letters, giving us a glimpse of his thoughts and goals, and depicting various facets of his personality. They also revealed a conflict of emotions at this stage of his education. His initial interest in missions was growing, due partly to the many letters he received from missionaries serving in various parts of the world. They wrote to their alma mater with news of their progress and requests for prayer. Through these, John gained insight into real-life situations on the field, rather than textbook missionology alone. But a delicate problem confronted him concerning his father's hopes and vision for his future. Peter Stam had gladly released his son to study at Moody, but he secretly harbored the wish that once his examinations were over, John would return home to take over the leadership of the Star of Hope Mission.

John was as familiar with the workings of the organization as his father, and had worked with some of the teams. Peter was getting older, and knew that he couldn't continue indefinitely; but the work was very dear to his heart, and did serve a real need in the community. Interestingly enough, Mr. Stam was very content to see another son do missionary work in Africa, but not so anxious for John to go. And although John did not necessarily share his father's conviction about his joining the Star of Hope, he was unsure about his future. He felt pulled in two directions.

"The Lord knows where he wants me," John wrote to his brother Jacob, anxious to follow the Lord's leading rather than family tradition. At the same time, he was reluctant to upset his father and spent much time in prayer over the matter, which was eventually rewarded when his father's attitude changed.

His very words later were: "May the Lord bless you and guide you by His Holy Spirit to d̶ ̶ ̶ ̶ ̶ ̶ ̶ will. We must pray that more men go to China."

A challenge to his missionary call was by no means peculiar to John Stam. Other candidates before him had been subject to such diversions, however well meant. C. T. Studd, the famous missionary explorer who served in China, India, and Africa, and who founded the Worldwide Evangelization Crusade, went through several intensely emotional scenes with his widowed mother before he finally received her blessing to go abroad.

John held the same conviction as a fellow countryman, Jim Elliot, who wrote twenty years later in his notebook, found after his death, mud-stained and sodden, on the Curaray Beach: "There is one Christian worker for every 50,000 people in foreign lands, while there is one to every 500 in the United States." It is interesting to note that both these men, single-minded in their devotion, were to lose their lives as twentieth-century martyrs. John expressed himself in slightly different words than Jim, but the message comes through the same: "It does look frightfully disproportionate to see so many here in comparison with the few over yonder."

Full-time Christian work in the United States would certainly have been an easier option, notwithstanding a demanding assignment in itself. Primarily, the language difficulty didn't exist, unless one was dealing with ethnic minorities. Disease, loneliness, lack of fellowship with other believers, and all other missionary deprivations were considerably lessened in home surroundings. And John would certainly have experienced full parental support from the first. Conditions in China were far from ideal in the summer of 1930. The province of Kiangsi had fallen largely into Communist hands. Even after conquest, peaceful conditions had not returned—pillage and murder of innocent civilians was the order of the day. And the carnage was not restricted to nationals—three associate members of the China Inland Mission had already been killed in the conflict, and two others were imprisoned by the enemy. These war-like conditions were surely enough to make missionary candidates rethink their future plans.

John kept abreast of developments there. He wrote to his brother details about the captured couple—Mr. and Mrs. R. W. Porteous, who were fortunately released after having been in the hands of the Communists for one hundred days. Rather than spend their captivity cowering in fear, they had witnessed and preached boldly to their captors. John was particularly impressed that the areas in China under attack at that time were the very ones where Mission effort had been intensified. It was obvious that the forces of evil were resisting in panic the rapid spread of the Gospel.

Another student, who had already spent a year at the Moody Bible Institute when John enrolled there, had grown up in completely different surroundings. The two first became aware of each other by their common interest in China—expressed by their attendance at a China Inland Mission prayer meeting held weekly in the home of a Mr. and Mrs. Isaac Page. The acquaintance—Elisabeth Alden Scott—took her middle name from her ancestors, John and Priscilla

Alden, of the Mayflower. Thus, her roots were firmly based in New England territory—perhaps explaining her courage, resoluteness, and determination which she displayed in the face of adversity and danger late in her life.

The Mayflower, as we know, set sail in 1620, its personnel consisting of "saints and strangers," according to the contemporary records. These were mostly churchmen who, tired of the pressure exerted on Christians who wanted to worship in their own way, set out for the New World where they could enjoy religious freedom. Some of the travelers were simply adventurers with itching feet who joined the expedition for the challenge and excitement. November 11 was the day they first set foot on the eastern shores of America. They had embarked at the worst possible time of the year, and the weather attested to that.

Governor William Bradford, to the benefit and interest of us all, kept a detailed journal. The first winter took its relentless toll. Illness struck so many, that it was difficult to find enough people well to tend the sick. At least half their number died. One of the biggest problems was finding enough basic foodstuffs— the vessels carrying supplies across the stormy Atlantic didn't arrive for months. It was a whole year before full relief arrived.

In his colorful and dramatic phraseology, Bradford wrote:

"If they looked behind them, there was the mighty ocean which they had crossed, and was now a main bar and gulf separating them from the civil world. What could now sustain them, but the Spirit of God and His grace? May not and ought not the children of these fathers rightly say, 'Our fathers were Englishmen who came over this great ocean, and were ready to perish in this wilderness; but they cried unto the Lord, and He heard their voice and looked on their adversity.' Let them therefore praise the Lord, because He is good and His mercies endure for ever."

He continued philosophizing:

"Thus out of small beginnings, greater things have been produced by His hand—that made all things of nothing—and gives being to all things that are; and as one small candle may light a thousand; so the light here kindled hath shone unto many. . . ."

Betty Scott Stam, herself a great word-spinner, would have appreciated that sonorous prose of Governor Bradford. The small candle of faith that was lit so long ago by the Mayflower settlers, including John and Priscilla Alden, beamed out across the world like a mighty beacon. In just the same way, about two hundred and fifty years later, the enduring flame kindled by John and Betty Stam in far-away China was not to be extinguished. Their names have become a byword among twentieth-century Christians for courage and selflessness. Although ordinary people in themselves, they were filled with the Spirit of God.

5

Betty Scott

*I*t was not from her ancestry alone that Betty Scott derived her early interest in the Christian faith. Her own parents were very much involved in missionary outreach when she was born. Dr. Charles Ernest Scott, her father, won acclaim as a notable scholar in a distinguished academic career before he decided to turn his back on the world of universities and colleges to begin home missionary work in Michigan. It was a less than glamorous, poorly paid, and unacclaimed task, but they persevered. Betty was born in the town of Albion, before her family set sail for a new sphere of service—this time, in China.

In the new land, as in his home country, Dr. Scott poured out all his energies in preaching, teaching and writing—to assure that Chinese men and women had a chance to hear about the one true God. Conditions were difficult, and the work strenuous, but—unlike Lot's wife—they never looked back.

In one of her lesser-known books, *These Strange*

Ashes, one-time missionary, and well-known author Elisabeth Elliot, paid tribute to the Scott household:

"From as far back as I can remember, I have been hearing about missionaries. My parents had been missionaries . . . missionaries stayed in our home, spoke at our church, and were very much part of our lives. Betty Scott Stam . . . had been one of the guests. Her father, Dr. Charles Ernest Scott, wrote to me when I was a little girl and sent me things from China—a paper fan, some tiger-skin slippers. They were interesting and romantic people. But besides this they were people of high and serious purpose. Their business was to go out and spread the Gospel. Spreading the Gospel meant missionary journeys like those of St. Paul related in the Book of Acts, when he went out preaching the Good News of the Resurrection."

Obviously, Betty's father was not only a notable scholar, but a caring father and friend. From experience he knew what pleased his own little daughter, and was willing to spend time and thought in the midst of a hectic schedule to send a parcel to another missionary child. No doubt he was aware, too, of how missionary children missed out on presents of toys and new clothing. Certainly Betty—eldest of the family of five—was devoted to him. They were a close-knit family unit with "togetherness" as their motto.

Perhaps their parents wanted to compensate them in their early years for the inevitable separation that would follow. First they lived in the seaside city of Tsingtao. They derived maximum pleasure from outings to the beach and to the lovely wooded countryside surrounding them. After Betty had left for boarding school near Peking, the family moved to Tsinan.

In spite of their main duties, the Scotts devoted as much time as possible to their children's upbringing. But it wasn't "all work and no play." Time was set aside for outdoor games and athletics, as well as for family prayers and reading children's books together. In all of this, the parents must have passed on their ideals to the children, because each one followed in their footsteps regarding their futures, when they became adults.

Dr. Courtenay T. Fen of the Presbyterian Board wrote later in a letter:

"Elisabeth and Beatrice have already gone to China . . . the former to lay down her life heroically with her husband; Beatrice, as the wife of Dr. Theodore Stevenson, is just beginning to work in our South China Mission. Helen is now under appointment with her husband, the Rev. George Gordon Mahy, Jr., after several years of service in the Witherspoon College, Kentucky. Francis, now a student in Princeton Seminary, and his younger brother Kenneth, in Davidson College, are also planning for the mission field."

It certainly wasn't an automatic decision that each of the children eventually took up missionary work. The reason why they followed their parents' example was that when they grew old enough to make up their own minds, they looked back with affection on their happy childhood and the firm but kindly discipline administered to them. It worked for them. They admired their parents' ideals and dedication to their Christian calling. Obviously they felt in no way deprived if they were prepared to bring their own families up similarly. Betty wasn't to know then how God would care for her baby in a crisis, but there must have been many times when she saw Him intervene in loving care in her own early years.

Betty was the first to leave home, but one by one the others joined her in a co-educational school. She was a popular pupil, but took time off from her own friendships to mother the younger members of her family who were perhaps feeling homesick. Twice a year they returned home, at Christmas and then for the long summer holidays, which they spent at their seaside cottage.

Sometimes Betty expressed her thoughts in writing verse. One poem, "To Father and Mother," gives a particular insight into her appreciation of her parents training:

> You loved and learned and stood beside us,
> And understood the shocks of youth . . .
> You fed my mind . . .
> You taught the Word and Way for sinners,
> Until Christ's Spirit brought me light . . .
> Your life for others, in each other,
> Shines through the world, pain-tarnished here.

With these precious, happy years behind them, the Scott family faced an even harder separation than boarding-school—when Betty reached seventeen, higher education in China just wasn't available. Happily, this watershed in her young life occurred as their next furlough was due. Her parents, probably realizing that the family would never remain completely together again, planned in advance an exciting itinerary embracing Egypt, Israel, Greece, Italy, Switzerland, France and England. It took six months of travel before they finally reached the United States of America, but their minds and hearts were full of new friends, experiences, and scenic beauty they had encountered on the way.

We are indebted to Betty's sister Helen for a description of their tour: "All of us kept voluminous diaries and were thrilled to the core by every fresh experience. Of course, the Holy Land was the most moving. . . ." Then she cited some outstanding impressions, such as Vesuvius, the Tombs of the Kings of Egypt, and St. Peter's in Rome. All these wonders of the modern world must have seemed in tremendous contrast to the Chinese culture to which they were accustomed.

As might be expected, Betty was again moved to write verse—"Traveler's Song"—to commemorate her tour, and pick out the highlights. Color always played a great part in her vocabulary. Later she wrote a poem entitled "Color," going through the whole spectrum as revealed in nature: blue Swiss lakes, an apple tree, a crimson rosebud, scarlet poppies, a scarlet lobelia plant, Kuamasa cardinal, waving yellow daffodils, the pearly pinkish lining of a shell.

None of the children regarded the separation from China as final: "We all expected to return as missionaries. Our parents never urged it, but it seemed the natural and right thing to do."

To smooth the transition from one culture to another, Dr. and Mrs. Scott stayed on in the States for a few extra months, when Betty was to remain for her schooling. It was fortunate they did, because after a short time there, Betty, usually so fit and active, succumbed to a very serious and painful illness. Rheumatic fever wreaked havoc on her constitution, and compelled her to lie flat in bed for months—with her heart considerably weakened by the strain. All concerned were glad that her parents were able to see her through this long convalescence. Another comfort for Betty was the pleasure she derived from writing her poetry, which helped to pass the time without exerting her physically.

By the time she entered Wilson College in Pennsylvania, she had, through her extensive travels and subsequent illness, acquired a new outlook on life, making her more mature than many of the students her age. She seemed to be on a different plain than her contemporaries, and found it difficult to communicate with them. It wasn't that she'd set herself up on a pedestal, but people viewed her as such, when they heard of her experiences. In time, her natural friendliness and thoughtfulness for others broke down the barriers, and when her sister Helen joined her a couple of years later, Betty was an individual of some standing in college. Helen wrote:

"She had been elected president of the literary society, associate editor of the literary publication, interested also in dramatics, and an active student volunteer. She was acknowledged to be one of the finest students in her class, graduating Magna Cum Laude . . . Betty was interested in everything I went out for, especially athletics, which her heart condition would not allow her to take up; and she rejoiced in my little victories even more than I did."

Obviously, with missionary parents, she had been acquainted with the facts of the Christian gospel from an early age. Wisely, her parents had put their family under no pressure to make a positive response. As children they attended no church or Sunday school, as the only option was a long Chinese service which would have proved completely unsuitable for them.

They probably learned more from their parents' example in the home than anywhere else. But at a summer conference in Keswick, New Jersey, during Betty's first long college vacation, it all came alive to her in a very special way. Writing to her parents, she explained her new-found happiness to them:

"Keswick is over, but I trust never the message! I have now surrendered myself to the Lord more than I have ever realized was possible . . . Among other things, I have dedicated to Him whatever I have of poetic or literary gift. Maybe He can use me along that line . . . Giving my life to Jesus makes me see what I ought to have done long ago, and I wonder how I could have been so dumb before . . . I don't know what God has in store for me. I really am willing to be an old-maid missionary, or an old-maid anything else, all my life, if God wants me to. It's as clear as daylight to me that the only worthwhile life is one of unconditional surrender to God's will, and living in His way, trusting His love and guidance."

Later, in writing her testimony for *China's Millions*, the official magazine of the China Inland Mission, she penned the following paragraphs:

"A missionary's daughter, brought up in China, I have always seen something of heathenism. But, although I knew the Lord as Savior so early that I cannot remember any definite decision, many experiences and battles followed before I truly accepted the Savior as my Lord.

"During my school years, I prayed that if it were God's will, nothing might prevent me from returning to China as a missionary. My parents and others prayed thus about me, too. I, myself, first made this prayer in 1925 at Keswick, where I received this verse, 'For to me to live is Christ, and to die is gain.' Since then, other lines of activity, even other fields, have come up before me—and I cannot say they were not of the Lord—while even as recent as September of this year, it was uncertain whether, for physical reasons, I would be accepted at all.

"But 'I being in the way, the Lord led me.' He, who made me willing to serve Him anywhere, has closed all other doors and opened this one—service under the China Inland Mission in China. For this I praise His name; for I love China and believe it is the neediest country—just now, needier than ever. I will make mention of His faithfulness, which is great. Praising the Lord is, I believe, the only thing in the world worth doing. And praising Him involves bringing in other members of His body—those now in heathenism—to Him."

Certainly, this was a clear statement of her goals and objectives. Above the article, in a row of four photographs of missionary candidates, Betty's solemn face appeared, with the caption: "Miss Elisabeth A. Scott, BA, daughter of Dr. and Mrs. C. E. Scott of Shantung, China." She wore large, round spectacles, and her hair was parted on the side and combed straight. She looked somewhat serious, but upon closer scrutiny, one will notice a half-smile on her face. She wore an attractive necklace and a plain, dark dress. The sense of humor with which she was blessed, and which came out strongly in several of her poems, is not apparent in this formal portrait.

6

A Common Purpose

*B*etty finished college with a firm conviction.
After her experience at Keswick, she knew
without a shadow of doubt that her main aim
in life was to return to China—the land of her childhood—as a missionary in her own right. Of course,
she only wanted to follow this plan of action in ac-
cordance with God's will, which she believed would
be made apparent as she worked and prayed to that
end. As her life's motto, she took the inspiring text
gleaned in the Keswick meetings: "For to me to live
is Christ, and to die is gain" (Phil. 1:21).

As she thought of the options before her, she con-
cluded that a course at the Moody Bible Institute
would best suit her needs for training. Her main objective, even at school, was to win souls for Christ,
not merely to be involved in theological discussion.
Her natural inclination was to remain in the background, rather than the foreground of evangelistic efforts. Like John, she was not at first prepared to ap-

proach strangers and present them with the claims of the Gospel. But in time, she managed to forget her own fears and inhibitions, and actually enjoyed unrehearsed encounters with needy people in the open-air.

Years later, when various friends paid tribute to her memory, they spoke of the traits of her personality that attracted them most to her. On the surface she was self-effacing, not at all extroverted. She took action only after serious thought and deliberation. Her manner of dress was plain and her hairstyle simple, but her facial features were soft and appealing and her voice had a melodious quality that was very pleasing to others. It was known that she spent a good deal of time in prayer. Even though the Keswick Conference sealed her direction for China, doubts crept in later. Was she choosing China as an easy option, a familiar culture and language for her? She was troubled about her indecision at times. Perhaps it was merely her own inclinations that were directing her thoughts to serve in her homeland. The plight of lepers suffering in Africa was very much on her heart for some time. Was it possible that the Lord was calling her, after all, to that dark continent and all the sacrifice that caring for lepers entailed?

Poems written at this time expressed her conflicting emotions on this important decision in her life. Poetry was her safety-valve for spiritual pressure. She could convey through her writing problems so personal that she could confide in no one else. Then when a particular struggle was over, and she had surrendered to the Lord without reservation, she would send some of her verses to her father to indicate what she had been going through and to what decision she had come:

> ... My child, I died for thee.
> And if the gift of love and life
> You took from Me,
> Shall I one precious thing withhold—
> ... My child, it cannot be.

Then sending a poem written slightly later, she explained that, "... the last stanza is His gracious acceptance of my unworthy self.":

> He answered me, and on his face
> A look ineffable of grace,
> Of perfect, understanding love,
> Which all my murmuring did remove.

After that, her doubts and indecision were resolved. Other problems might, and did in time arise, but her objective was fixed.

It was at this stage of Betty's spiritual journey that John's and her paths were destined to meet. John enrolled as a student when Betty had completed her first year. John's tall frame soon attracted her attention as he strode around the campus. Betty's quiet nature and modest appearance did not stand out in a crowd of classmates, and a quick glance at her would not attract immediate attention, but they did meet on common ground at the weekly prayer meeting for China. The Pages, who had already served in China and were acting as the mission's representatives in the Midwest, hosted the group in their home. The prayer time was always followed by coffee and conversation, and John was soon made aware of Betty's infectious enthusiasm for the cause. Without claiming that it was love at first sight, it wasn't long before John was taking a more than ordinary interest in her.

Unfortunately, there were obstacles that barred the way to an early understanding between them. John's every penny was accounted for to provide his basic daily needs; and to supplement his meager resources, his spare time was taken up with small jobs. The course of study itself was very exacting, demanding concentration of mind and effort. So time and finances were at a premium.

Beyond studies and work, John had pledged himself to carry out the duties of pastor to a small rural community. This added responsibility required a trip of two hundred miles from Chicago to Ohio—a journey he undertook once or twice a month. But John's sacrifice of time and money did not go unregarded. When writing later about his pastoral visits, the people of Elida, Ohio, were extremely appreciative of his ministry:

"We shall always remember John's first appearance in our pulpit, and how pleased we were with his earnest message. His kind, courteous manner, his zeal and fresh enthusiasm, and his helpful sermons won us completely. His remuneration was very little, yet his interest in and affection for us were greater than the difficulties, and he remained our faithful pastor until he graduated from the Bible Institute."

To John it was certainly not a wearisome chore. There must have been times when he felt tired and pressured with the combination of church work, studies and secular jobs. Yet he derived a great deal of pleasure from the fellowship and hospitality enjoyed on the weekends. Even though they were far from sophisticated, he enjoyed the eagerness and openness of these simple country folk. He found it a veritable tonic to leave the vast inner-city of Chicago—a sprawling giant even in those days—and stroll out under the starry skies where he could absorb the beauty of the heavens, unimpeded by city blocks and skyscrapers; no litter beneath his feet, just the fresh green turf. A member of the congregation wrote:

"These walks often involved visits to all kinds of people in need in the community, whether evangelical Christians, Catholics, or unbelievers. He tried to bring others into the happy fellowship of the church, who normally did not attend any services.

"John was one of the finest young men. He loved his Bible and loved to tell of Jesus . . . to come to the country and see God's wonderful handiwork in nature. He loved children, and would teach them Bible stories and choruses."

John's tenor voice was always in demand. Sometimes other students joined him for the weekend, and formed a singing quartet to add variety to the program.

"John was more than our minister. He not only taught and preached, he was our close and intimate friend. He visited most, if not all of us, in our homes. He was quick to see a joke and could be happy and enjoy himself wherever he happened to be, especially so where there were young folks and children. And they loved him greatly . . . Best of all, he made the Word of God live for us. Faithfulness was a theme he loved to dwell upon. . . ."

John devised various means of trying to "fix" Bible passages in people's hearts. For a change, he would sometimes organize a quarter of an hour of reciting Scripture from memory before the sermon. This habit would stand him in good stead one day when he was deprived of his Bible. Certain texts seemed particularly precious to him, including, "My God shall supply all your need according to his riches in glory by Christ Jesus" (Phil. 4:19).

For quite a long while, John shared with no one the decision that he made concerning his financial affairs when starting college. He wanted to prove practically for himself the plan he had thought through. In the spring of 1931, however, he sent a long letter to his father indicating how the Lord had blessed and helped him since he had decided to rely on God alone.

"And the Lord has wonderfully shown himself to me as Jehovah-jireh (the Lord will provide). Some time, perhaps, just before I leave for China, I may tell you some of these experiences. How I do thank Him for this past year! I would not have had it otherwise for all the ease of a bank balance."

It would be believed by all who knew his character that John wrote that letter to his father in all sincerity, not at all boasting of spirituality.

John always kept in close touch with home, writing regularly to his father, or brothers and sisters. He was anxious to hear news about the Star of Hope Mission, even though he was not called himself to work in that area. The claims of China pressed heavily upon him. "A million a month pass into Christless graves over there . . . God can use us if only we are empty, broken vessels in His hands."

The new relationship that was developing between him and Betty brought both joys and perplexities. They seemed so at one in their thoughts, aspirations and ambitions that it seemed hard not to imagine that God had brought them together for a special purpose. Yet the prospect of marrying Betty, however naturally pleasing, conflicted with his earlier plans. He had imagined that he would travel to China as a single man and probably remain as such for a minimum of five years. If he was to become involved in pioneer evangelistic work, it would mean a tough and difficult way of life—certainly not suited to a woman, particularly one with small children. This advancing thrust of the Mission excited him with its prospect of souls being saved in areas hitherto unreached by the Gospel.

Betty, however shy, was the last person to be coy about their relationship. She was too honest to pretend that she did not care for John in a special way, but the timing of an engagement just then did not seem appropriate. Betty, being one year ahead of him in college, had applied to the China Inland Mission as a candidate and, if all went as expected, she would be sailing in a few months. Another year of college, now seeming a long time indeed, stretched ahead for John. He would most likely be accepted for service in China, but it was certainly not automatic. He would need to pass medical exams and an aptitude test before the missions board.

The beginning of the 1930's was not an affluent era by any standards. America was still in the throes of a depression, and financial and other resources

were scarce. Missionary societies typically func-
tioned through the sacrificial giving of their support-
ers. John, of course, had very little material goods to
offer Betty, and they couldn't be sure what the year
ahead would bring. There was always the possibility,
however remote, that John would not be accepted by
the Mission. Since Betty was set apart for China, and
ready to go, they both felt they should proceed with
their individual lives. Each had dedicated themselves personally to God, and neither felt they could
at this stage claim what did not belong to them.

7

To China—at Last

Arrangements were made for Betty to sail for China in the autumn of 1931. In those days, air travel was a luxury enjoyed by very few. The normal way of intercontinental travel remained by sea. It was a very slow journey, but it gave at least one advantage to missionary candidates—instead of being hurtled within a few short hours from one culture to another, they had time to reflect and prepare themselves for the new life ahead with all its many changes.

Mercifully for the two young people, Betty was able to spend a full day in Chicago with John in the midst of her tight schedule. The hours slipped by all too quickly by the lake, as they talked and prayed together. It was a Monday, the day of the prayer meeting in the home of Mr. and Mrs. Page, which came as a fitting ending to their time together. John was able to confide in the Pages, as long-time and valued friends, what their hopes were for the future. No engagement was imminent, but each had complete confidence in the other and had committed their very precious relationship to God for His keeping.

In writing about his relationship with Betty to his parents, John was afraid that it may sound to them very prosaic and businesslike, and that their feelings weren't involved. He worded it the best he could: "We're ordinary young people, very much in love with each other, but wanting to put God first in our lives. We do care deeply about each other, be sure of that."

John's father understood perfectly when he received the letter. He said, "Those children are going to have God's choicest blessing! When God is second, you will get second-best; but when God is really first, you have His best." And what better valedictory message could Betty receive for the start of her new work in China? "Seek ye first the kingdom of God, and His righteousness; and all these things shall be added unto you" (Matt. 6:33).

In spite of the excitement of the sea voyage and the satisfaction of knowing she had prepared herself well for service, Betty felt the strain of parting with John, especially having no formal engagement to seal their relationship.

She had already spent eight months in China before John came to the end of his studies at Moody Bible Institute, and although Betty was returned to a country where she had grown up and made many friends, she was there in a new capacity with its own adjustments. The standards she set for herself were high, owing to the example her parents had been of unselfish commitment to the good of the Chinese people.

The months of concentration on his studies had

helped John through the loneliness of being apart from Betty. Now he had applied to the China Inland Mission, and would soon be assessed as a candidate by the director and council. Weeks of uncertainty lay ahead before he would know the outcome. Medical exams were also yet to be made.

In the days of final institute exams, John was chosen by his fellow students to deliver the class address at their graduation ceremony. Characteristically, he gave it a good deal of thought and preparation. He wasn't content to merely deliver a smooth, polished oration but rather to speak on a subject dear to his heart, and which he hoped would move others. He coupled the class motto, "Bearing Precious Seed," with the text, "The field is the world." In his mind's eye, John envisioned the many doors still open to the Gospel in various parts of the world. How many would remain open for long? Some had already ominously closed.

". . . Heathen populations are growing in numbers daily, but we are not reaching them. Now is the time to reach men whose minds are swept of old beliefs— before Communistic Atheism, coming in like a flood, raises other barriers far harder to overcome—and before this generation passes into Christless graves."

He attacked the inroads of humanism into the educational system and the breaking down of the old standards of morality. The Christian church lacked joy and power, he felt. Activities were being held up through lack of financial support. "Shall we beat a retreat or dare we advance at God's command in face of the impossible?" was his final question. A sober and almost prophetic comment completed that section of his speech: "We are told to expect tribulation and even persecution, but with it victory in Christ."

One could assume that John was very spiritually minded, perhaps impractical, but spontaneous comments from his classmates give balance to his character: "John was not ascetic in any way. He was plenty of fun on a trip or at a picnic—a regular fellow, if ever there was one." Others mentioned his cheerful countenance and manner, his hearty handshake.

On July 1, 1932, John was officially accepted as a candidate by the China Inland Mission. He had already stayed six weeks at their Philadelphia headquarters. Declining with regret an offer to go on a cruise to Bermuda with Christian friends, not feeling he could indulge himself while other missionaries suffered privations, he crossed the States by car and, together with five other young men and two returning missionaries, sailed on the *Empress of Japan*, stopping at Honolulu and Japan.

Before the long awaited trip, however, John wrote Betty to test her reaction to the mention of an official engagement, feeling now a certain freedom with his future set to be shared on the same soil and with the same mission as Betty.

But no answer came—not even a scribbled note. Had he placed too much hope on an affirmative answer? Had she changed her mind in the intervening months? He had always said that to follow the will of God was his greatest desire, but if this involved losing Betty, how prepared was he to accept that disappointment? With no firm news, these questions jumbled through his mind, causing him considerable anxiety even though he was so close to reaching the land of his calling. Surely something out of the ordinary must have happened.

On her arrival in China, Betty was posted to Fowyang in northern Anhwei. She was delighted to find
that, in spite of several years absence, she could soon
recall much of the language she had learned as a
child. Unfortunately, she and all other women missionaries were instructed to leave the area, because
Communist guerrillas had kidnapped the senior missionary, Mr. H. S. Ferguson, and no reliable evidence
was ever discovered about his fate. It was especially
difficult to leave the Chinese Christians to whatever
fate might befall them.

Betty's parents who were returning from furlough
asked her to meet them at the docks in Shanghai.
Delighted to be reunited with them again, she hur-
riedly made the trip there only to be disappointed
when their arrival was delayed several days. When
at last they docked, she made the trip again from her
temporary station, but was stricken with tonsillitis
which kept her in Shanghai for several weeks' treatment. God had His own way of answering prayer and
bringing matters to a happy conclusion.

When the *Empress of Japan* docked, John was overjoyed to discover that Betty was still in Shanghai.
The confusion about the missing letter that had gone
to her old address was soon cleared up and no obsta-
cle remained to prevent their engagement. Their happiness was infectious and their news spread rapidly
around to all the staff at headquarters, evoking a positive response.

Sadly, the happy couple had to part again, and
were destined not to see each other until just before
their marriage a year later. Betty, escorted by Mr. and
Mrs. Glittenberg, returned to Fowyang. John traveled
by the slower means of steamer on the Yangtze, his

objective being the language school of the China Inland Mission where he was to join up with a group of about thirty other young men. After spending barely a week with Betty, he was still ecstatic with happiness as he wrote from on board to his family at home in Paterson, all eager for news.

"I still cannot cease praising the Lord and wondering at his goodness in bringing Betty to Shanghai and keeping her there until I came! One of the boys from Australia asked me how we had 'worked' it, and it was just blessed to realize that we hadn't worked it at all. It was unplanned and unexpected, as far as we were concerned . . . Mr. Gibb, the China director, told me that he did not see any reason why we could not be married when my year of language school is up. To me it has been a wonderful illustration of the fact that when we do 'seek first' the kingdom of God, although our efforts may be blundering, He does faithfully add the 'all things.' "

Although Betty and John were both living in the same province, the mighty River Yangtze lay between them, dividing areas of different cultures, geographical features and weather. Betty, in the dry northwestern area, was amazed to find what a far-reaching work of God had been in progress when she arrived there. For the previous few years after the uprisings in 1925 no foreign missionaries had been allowed to remain in that area, so it was generally imagined that Christianity had fallen into a decline. The reverse was true. In the city of Fowyang, two hundred and fifty people met regularly on Sundays, with several baptisms and about eighty taking part in the Communion service. Even in the out-stations the work was flourishing to the astonishment of European missionaries, rather like a much later situation in China after the Cultural Revolution had taken its toll of believers. The very pressure of events had put new determination and stamina into them. Throughout the whole district a spirit of revival hovered. The main need was for teachers to instruct the young flock, so when Mr. and Mrs. Glittenberg arrived to take over from the Hamiltons, they were eagerly welcomed. Nancy Rodgers, who ran the girls' school, gave a warm welcome to Betty and her friend Katie Dodd. Back in the 1930's particularly, women missionaries were almost totally concerned with the evangelization of native women, and Betty was very keen to be involved in this as soon as possible. It was a work that suited her personality completely.

A highlight of the year was the autumn conference in Fowyang city, which was attended by hundreds of Christians from many different places. Betty quoted an approximate figure of eight hundred present. Later, eighty-two baptisms took place. With so many fresh openings for pastoral work and so much eagerness on the part of the people for teaching from the missionaries, little time remained for the purpose of language study. Usually this was rated as a priority in the early days of the first term of service, but Betty, with her unusual background of already possessing a working knowledge of the dialect, was soon plunged into person-to-person contacts. She was even able to take one trip outside the city to evangelize before the autumn conference.

8

The First Year's Service

*I*n an amusing letter home to her youngest brother, Betty described this trip in some detail. Her gift of language was very evident in her colorful and graphic descriptions. Humorous touches abounded; her letters were certainly far from boring or heavy:

"Whenever a little donkey trotted by, it raised a cloud of dust which could be seen for miles . . . When the flies saw us, they were tickled pink and headed straight for us! So did the people! . . . The rats bothered Katie, so she hauled her bedding down the ladder and slept on some benches. I stayed up above, but got a raft of smaller things than rats—ai-yah! Mock dismay!"

But it wasn't always a description of unwelcome visitors. Betty was always able to beautifully describe the color around her: ". . . a bunch of brilliant red peppers, hanging up today against a wall, persimmon trees, turning color so that every leaf is a different hue, ranging from all oranges and reds to green."

It was envisaged that at some stage Betty and Katie would live there and carry on a work among the women and children. Betty was always in her element when she was involved with children. She loved their innocent ways and recognized their potential. It was a challenge to get through to them with the message of the gospel before they grew up and adopted sinful habits and the worship of ancient gods:

"Some among them were the most precious little children you ever saw—really lovable unspoiled ones, whose eyes just shone, and who crowded around us and repeated every word we said, every verse and chorus, line by line, for hours."

Betty reveled in their undivided attention. No doubt the children enjoyed the novelty of these gentle foreign women anxious to teach them. Coming largely from peasant homes with hardworking mothers who had little time for anything but the daily grind of hard, manual chores, they appreciated learning Bible stories and singing lively hymns and choruses. But it wasn't only the little ones who flocked to the meetings, Betty explained to John in a letter:

"Oh, John, how the people streamed in yesterday after our arrival! . . . there were the loveliest young girls, besides crowds of women, students and children . . . How we long to start Bible classes for these educated girls, and other meetings for the women and children!"

Betty's vision grew with the opportunities all around her.

John eagerly awaited each letter and then read and reread them, devouring the news. Although Betty seemed quite well following her health problems in Shanghai, she was pushing herself relentlessly on a tiring schedule. With so many opportunities on every hand, there was little time for relaxation or ordinary rest periods. And although Betty had lived in China for many years as a child, it was in a Western-type home with American cooking, and certain standards of comfort, however modest. In Fowyang this was not the case. In fact, it was much like living in a goldfish bowl, particularly in the country districts: "We retired into a little inner room of a mud house (the inn) and there the people rushed us as though we were a couple of footballs. The landlady shoved them out bodily but they sneaked in anyway, until they were three deep all around us." Methods of hygiene were primitive: ". . . she left us with chopsticks in almost total darkness, not even able to see whether we were eating any of the flies!"

John's chief concern for Betty was the presence of bandits in the area. One or two incidents came to his attention, which gave basis to his fear. The first happened when Mrs. Glittenberg was compelled to take her baby Lois to a hospital, a day's journey by bus. Bandits waved down the bus and ordered all the passengers out, commandeering every piece of luggage. Little Lois's medicine and a few other necessities were packed in her mother's bag. In spite of her pleading, the soldiers were adamant and refused to return it. When finally Mrs. Glittenberg was able to hire a rickshaw and reach the hospital, it was too late, and the baby died there of dysentery. It was more than probable that the delay en route made the difference between life and death, but the authorities showed little concern.

On another occasion, first a couple of soldiers and later two companies comprising sixty men took up their quarters in the girls' school where Betty and Katie also had rooms. In Mr. Glittenberg's absence, the Chinese evangelist Mr. Ho tried to explain the situation to an important official. Eventually the men were lined up and marched off, much to the jubilation of the missionaries who had been praying earnestly. Fortunately, no harm was done on this occasion, but people regarded it as a straw in the wind. Who could tell if the outcome of future visits by the soldiers would be so harmless? They could only keep a watch on events and pray.

John passed on news of this and other happenings in a letter to his parents:

"The above will help you to pray more understandingly for her—for us both when we get out into the work. One never knows what one may run into. But we do know that the Lord Jehovah reigns . . . If we should go on before, it is only the quicker to enjoy the bliss of the Savior's presence."

In addition to his concern about Betty, he found the language study difficult, although he tackled it with his usual dedication and cheerfulness. He and the other students managed to keep fit by participating together in sports on the college campus. They were warned against going out together in the streets to avoid the suspicion that may arise at the sight of so many young foreign men in the city.

John's application to his studies paid off. By March 18 he was able to write:

"Hurrah! this morning I finished the last of the three language exams. I have taken one a day for three days . . . Then Saturday I am to lead morning worship in Chinese . . . When we first came out, and read what Hudson Taylor said about men preaching in Chinese six months after beginning to study, we smiled. But here it is—one day more than five months, and I have actually taken morning prayers! Praise the Lord!''

John went on to explain that the early training on the streets of his home town had stood him in good stead when he had to face that ordeal. Apparently some of his message got through, although he had to ask the pastor to pray in Chinese. The next important decision to be made was his future location of work. With fifteen provinces now available in mainland China, as well as outlying provinces, the field was a wide one and all the students awaited anxiously the arrival of the general director, Mr. Hoste, who would interview each candidate personally.

Two accounts exist of John's meeting with Mr. Hoste, one in the book by Mrs. Howard Taylor and the other from the August 1933 edition of the Mission magazine, *China's Millions*. No doubt each of the young men felt a little apprehensive about the outcome which would decide their future for the next few years. Who would be their fellow-workers with whom they were expected to labor in close harmony? They were all servants of the Lord, anxious to please the same Master—but personalities did matter. It was important to be assigned to work with someone compatible, if they were to pull together under the same yoke.

Then, too, for most of them it was their first encounter with Dixon Edward Hoste, an almost legendary figure by this time, who had sailed out to China in February 1885 as one of the original "Cambridge Seven" with C. T. Studd. The Cambridge Seven consisted of seven wealthy young men of social standing who all became missionaries to China. Dixon Hoste had originally been destined for a career in the army, and had been serving with his battery as a lieutenant in the Isle of Wight when his brother William returned home from Trinity College for Christmas vacation. He had been greatly affected by the spirit of revival which had been sweeping through Cambridge, and was eager to win his younger brother Dixon for Christ.

Dixon's conversion, however, was far from automatic and immediate. Brought up rather severely by orthodox Christian parents, he had never shown any eagerness for a lively faith. Fortunately, his brother was not easily discouraged, and at length managed to get him to attend a Moody and Sankey Mission in Brighton. Dixon struggled with his conscience for two weeks before finally walking to the front in answer to Moody's appeal.

This proved to be no fleeting, emotional reaction. Within a short time he was testifying, "This experience has changed my life; I want to make it known where Christ is not known. There are many people in other lands who have never heard the Gospel, and the Lord wants them to hear it, for He says so. I want to give my life to this." His father wisely counseled him not to resign his commission immediately but give himself time to plan his future.

Dixon's witness to his fellow officers struck everyone as most sincere, even if they did not share his convictions. By May, his father had given him leave to make a break from the Army, convinced that this spiritual fervor was going to last. Meanwhile, he had received literature from his brother about the C.I.M. "Can the Christians of England sit still with folded arms while these multitudes are perishing?" was his comment. He was interviewed by Hudson Taylor, lately returned from China, in London. Although Hudson, like his father, warned him of the difficulties of work in that country, Dixon left the mission headquarters with an even greater desire to serve the Lord in China.

When he finally set sail in 1885 with the team, little could he foretell what the future held for him in China. He worked for many years in Shansi with Pastor Hsi and succeeded Hudson Taylor as head of C.I.M. in 1903. He held that post for the next thirty years, retiring in 1935. Remaining in Shanghai, he was interned by the Japanese in 1944 and left China the following year in a very weak state, more than sixty years after he had first set foot in the country. Just over six months later, in May 1946, he died in London, the last of the Cambridge Seven.

It was in 1933 that he interviewed John Stam. John explained in a letter that Mr. Hoste was compelled to stay in bed with a cold, so the interview took place in his bedroom.

"When you see Mr. Hoste under ordinary circumstances, his massive pointed beard and perfectly erect figure proclaim the fact that he was formerly an army officer. But it is quite different when you see him in bed, propped up with pillows . . . he looked more like a tired patriarch, ready to lay his burdens down. He just made me think of Jacob, leaning on his staff, blessing his sons."

Of course, the decisions of placement were not arbitrary. Much thought and prayer had gone before throughout the preceding few months. The young men were consulted at each stage. In such small mission stations it was essential to fit the right person into the right team. A square peg in a round hole would have thrown the whole project out of gear.

John was particularly impressed by the way Dixon Hoste prayed audibly for him and for Betty.

"I could not help feeling that this was not so much just a bowing of the head to ask the Lord to bless our deliberations, but that, when he began to pray, he forgot that I had come to be designated and was on his most important work, that of intercession . . . The outcome is that I am to go to Suangcheng for further study and start in the work with Mr. and Mrs. Birch from North America. Then it is intended that we open a new station in a city called Tsingteh."

It seemed there was already a growing church in Suancheng, which lay in the south of the province in picturesque mountainous country.

In the magazine article interview, John dwelt less on his time with Dixon Hoste and more on his own emotions and reactions.

"The Lord has abundantly answered prayer in regard to the studies. Never have I been more conscious that folk have been praying for me, and while at first it certainly did look like a frightful language to learn, yet the Lord gave understanding and interest, and helped me to remember—so much so that in less than five months I passed the first section examination; and in one day more than five months had the privilege of leading Chinese morning prayers for the first time. If you have never tried to speak in a new language before a crowd, you do not know what it feels like, but while I was not perhaps as cool as usual, my heart was full of praise to the Lord that He had given me ability to get at least some little bit of His Word across to the people. With so small a vocabulary as we still have it is far from easy to express oneself. That morning as we were singing the opening hymn,

I thought again of the words of the Lord Jesus, 'For this cause came I unto this hour,' and realized that for me too, all the background of life and training has been to prepare me for this hour—a thought which has often helped me in difficult places."

John was to quote this text again later in the greatest crisis of his life.

"On Monday our general director, Mr. Hoste, arrived for the designations. Eighteen of the twenty-five of us did not know where we were going, and you can imagine the interest and suspense. As each came back from his interview the rest would want to know where he was to be sent.

"For the present I am designated to Suancheng, Anhwei Province. Ningkwo is the old name which you will probably have to look for on the map. I am to be there for some time engaged in language study, and in getting my start in the work. After that it is intended that we should open Tsingteh, a new station to the southwest, so if I am not a member of The Two Hundred[1], it looks as if I shall go into Forward Movement work after all. Praise the Lord."

Referring to the "we" in reference to the work in Tsingteh, would indicate that he and Betty would serve in that area after they were married.

---

[1] In 1911 a special appeal went out from C.I.M. for two hundred people to volunteer as missionaries for China. Those who answered that call were always known as "The Two Hundred."

9

The Wedding

As an initial bonus, John was given the summer months of 1933 for study. True to his tradition of putting self and his own comfort and convenience last, he refused to accept an invitation to live by the seacoast to escape the intense summer heat. It was a similar gesture to the one he made when he declined a cruise with Christian friends to Bermuda but sailed third-class on the *Empress of Japan* on his way to China. Perhaps gesture is the wrong word. It was a deliberate decision to choose a course of action which he believed would best further the gospel, although deprive himself of a well-earned chance for relaxation.

Traveling direct to his new locality, he arrived in Suancheng to be welcomed by Mr. Birch. John made an immediate impression on his host, with his tall frame, hearty handshake, happy smile, and uprightness of character. But it wasn't just a physical impression—it was soon apparent that "John lived with God and loved to talk of things that were filling his heart." John was so glad to be nearing his goals at last. Already he was an accepted member of the China Inland Mission, having passed his first course of language study, and within a few short months he would be married to Betty and working in close harmony with her.

But a further test of stamina soon awaited him. Mr. and Mrs. Birch planned to go to the hills for a very necessary change, and John was left in sole charge of the work. Although he had spent only eight months in China, he carried out as full a program as possible, even preaching in Chinese. Fortunately, his sense of humor stood him in good stead. "People laugh at my Chinese!" he remarked cheerfully in a letter to a friend. He was realistic about his linguistic abilities, always carrying around with him some gospel portions or tracts to give away. He would like to have followed them through more closely but felt at least his hearers had received a short message. He mentioned honestly in a letter that he was "tinged with blue one day" and felt greatly cheered by a good long letter from home.

Life had its ups and downs—difficult to sort out with a limited knowledge of the dialect. Talking about all the petty irritations of life that may crop up from day to day, John wrote, "The goat may die, thieves may come in and turn the compound into a place for a midnight manhunt. There may be plenty of interruptions and difficulties of one kind or another, but through it all has been the steady consciousness of the Lord's presence." Quite often, he realized, people came more for the novelty of seeing

a white man and listening to the gramophone, un-
heard of until now in this part of the world, than to
drink in the message.

Most of all, he tried to build bridges with people,
to offer them friendship and a genuine interest in
their affairs. He would go out for a stroll and drop in
at shops where he would linger for a chat and perhaps sometimes a chance to pass on a piece of literature. Another path he took frequently led him outside the city gates, or even to perch on the city wall
and gaze at the night sky and the beauty of the surrounding mountain ranges. It served as therapy for
John. "It's like a benediction and a choir singing an-
thems and a wonderful sermon all rolled into one,"
was how he described it. Practical as ever, he spent
time in gardening before breakfast to keep himself in
good physical condition, and even managed to put
in store sixty quarts of jams and preserves for Mrs.
Birch's return. Once these tasks were accomplished,
he tackled the second part of his language study, determined to finish that before he joined Betty in August in preparation for their wedding later in the year.

His patience and perseverance were slowly but
inevitably reaping their reward. People started drop-
ping in for a chat of their own accord, and one group
set aside a regular time for Bible study. The children
were a great joy when they came for their classes; he
found it very rewarding to teach them texts and scripture choruses, and he had great faith that adults listening to their singing might learn the truths of the
gospel, even though he couldn't express them adequately in their dialect. Altogether, he seemed remarkably free of tension in spite of the fierce heat

and the months on his own in a strange country. His ability to derive enjoyment from encounters with friendly people and the glory of nature plus his down-to-earth approach to tackling routine chores all helped him to adjust to an unfamiliar situation and environment.

As the day approached for his journey by steamer and train to reach Dr. and Mrs. Scott's home in Tsinan, his letter to his family in New Jersey resembled more of a psalm of praise than an ordinary newsletter. He listed all the blessings he had received up to that time but kept the best until last, "I shall soon be returning, God willing, with my wife—I like that phrase too!"

Fortunately, meeting Betty's family again did not prove as formidable an ordeal as it might have. He had already spent time with Betty's parents on his first arrival in Shanghai. According to Betty, "Mother just took to him from the very first. Daddy doesn't say so much, but he feels pretty good about it too." John's sense of humor and friendly, unassuming manner soon won their love and approval. Betty even laughingly commented that her mother would have given her no peace until she had said yes to John's proposal of marriage, even if she hadn't wanted him! They were all glad to have a short quiet time together before the hectic wedding arrangements gathered pace and the other guests began to arrive.

It would appear that everyone had decided that a full traditional wedding was appropriate even under the circumstances of bride and groom serving as missionaries in a foreign country and no detail was spared. Obviously Betty's mother enjoyed to the full her part in the organization. The gift of a beautiful day for the occasion, warmer than it had been (it was October 25, and well into the cool of autumn), and free of wind and dust, made her particularly thankful to God. They had planned an open-air ceremony, converting the tennis court into a temporary chapel, with rugs covering the floor and masses of flowers and potted plants banked up either side of the aisle. Even the autumnal tints of the ivy climbing up the south wall added color to the festive scene. Betty chose Katherine Dodd and Nancy Rodgers, her colleagues from Fowyang as her bridesmaids, together with Marguerite Luce, a former college friend and missionary nurse from Chefoo, as her maid of honor. Percy Bromley, a classmate from the language school, was John's best man. The Rev. A. Torrey, son of a well-known evangelist, conducted the service.

A black-and-white photograph printed in the February 1935 edition of *China's Millions* hardly does justice to the colorful occasion described in the book. Betty wore white silk crepe, trimmed with Brussels lace at the neck of the dress and the front of her veil. Their expressions in the photo revealed that they were perhaps overawed by the official photographing, but in the ceremony itself, they had eyes only for each other, and happy open smiles—not unusual for a Western-style wedding. (But the effect upon the Chinese guests was profound. Tradition dictates that the Chinese bride keep her eyes fixed on the ground, her head bowed in a sorrowful and fearful attitude.) The bridesmaids wore lavender silk, their bouquets of bright yellow chrysanthemums bound with wide yellow ribbons. Mention was made in the service about the manner of life and total commitment to the Lord of these two young people. Three quarters of the two hundred present were Chinese Christians, many of whom commented afterward on the benefit they received from the message. A wedding meal was served and then a short time of evening worship was held before the bride and groom left for a honeymoon in Tsingtao, where Betty had lived as a child.

Another wedding, another young couple to live happily ever afterward—or so it must have seemed to all the guests and family. As Christians, they knew in theory that life was uncertain, and the young pair had placed themselves unreservedly in the Lord's hands—but at this stage no one could have foretold the brevity of this marriage. Many were impressed by the consecration of John and Betty to the Lord's service, and a great future in the Mission was expected of them. But the harvest of souls they would reap for Him in the future would be brought about not so much by the manner of their life, but by their untimely death.

John's letter home after only two days of married bliss was predictably bubbly and overflowing with praise and thanksgiving. He wanted to make a permanent record "on some typewriter around here, before our blessings pile up so high that I may forget some of them." The beautiful autumn weather continued, enhancing the scenery of that seaside, mountainous area. Obviously they were on cloud nine. "I am sure none of the boys (his brothers) has had so lovely a honeymoon as Betty and I are having." Returning to base after such a glorious two weeks might have seemed rather dulling, particularly as they were soon immersed in language study again, but the magic was still working.

Meals were shared with the Birches to economize in time and effort while they were still studying, but they had their own rooms in the Mission compound. True to the example of the Mission's founder, Hudson Taylor, they equipped themselves with Chinese clothing to face the long, cold winter ahead. "You ought to see John in his fur-lined gown! He looks taller than ever. It is something to watch him gather his arms up under the skirts in the back when he is going downstairs, for all the world like an old Chinese gentleman!" Betty commented with amusement.

Song, the tailor, not only fitted them with a complete Chinese wardrobe, but also accompanied John and Betty on the first trip they took together to an out-station. It would have been easy to become so engrossed in language study so as to have very few outside contacts with other Christians. Both John and Betty were aware of the problem, however, and organized their time as equally as possible between language work and evangelism. John recognized the caliber of the local Christians. "I do thank the Lord for bringing me to this station, for there are many fine Christians here. . . ."

Far from feeling superior to the uneducated Chinese, John felt humbled in their presence when he witnessed their way of life. It was not only costly to be a Christian in China in those days, it was positively dangerous, yet they were fearless in following God's law. "Song gives whole weeks of his time going out over the country preaching . . . He closes his shop on Sundays, paying his five assistants the same as ever, and bringing them to church with him . . . his competitors think it is pure loss, but Song knows better and praises the Lord that his business prospers."

It was all the more remarkable that these "fine Christians" had only recently turned to God from the worship of idols.

10

A Missionary Journey

*T*he expedition to Swenchiapu was accomplished by four hours of walking, but this included many conversations along the way. The return trip took two hours longer but no one complained. "It was really delightful," was John's comment. They even managed to fit in an open-air meeting en route and were only too glad that they had given away every piece of literature in their possession.

Both Betty and John rejoiced in the many opportunities that had arisen for one-on-one encounters with inquirers curious to know more of the Gospel, and also the whole Sunday program, beginning with a worship service followed by Communion. A packed schedule followed for the rest of the day—another chapel meeting, two crowded open-air rallies and finally a large congregation to address back in the chapel. They had been encouraged, too, by the depth of the Christian family with whom they had stayed.

Betty had accompanied Mrs. Pao on walks around the town to chat with women and children in between the services. Pao, at some cost to himself, had followed Song's example in keeping Sunday free of work. Contrary to his business rival's expectations, he had cleared a large debt in spite of losing one trading day a week, and God had miraculously kept his premises safe when a fierce fire threatened the area.

The next trip they made was six times longer, taking a southwesterly direction from Suancheng. They tackled this at the Chinese New Year in February 1934, when an annual holiday was held. They were particularly anxious to become acquainted with this region, for it was in the little city of Tsingteh where they hoped to work next. Betty's account, published in the August 1934 edition of *China's Millions*, gave a graphic description of the area. The article was entitled "A Preliminary Survey."

"Tsingteh is a pathetic-looking city, set in the valley among splendid mountains. Pathetic from without, because it has a large, rambling city wall, and comparatively few houses; only acres of overgrown tangle, vegetable garden, and mulberry orchards where people used to be. Pathetic from within, because you see in closer view the crumbling ruins of wealthy palaces, and the broken bricks piled up like stones for the walls of poor people. This country was almost entirely depopulated during the T'aiping (Mighty Peace) Rebellion, and here are the crumbling palaces of the proud Chinese nobles! Some blamed these troubles upon the fact that in one place the city wall reared up into a corner resembling a turtle's head—an unlucky omen, but too late now to change.

"All that is left to remind us of proud, old families, whose representatives attended the Emperor, are the ancestral temples, features quite common to Central and South China, where pride of race and blood runs deeper and higher than in the more mongrel North. There can hardly be a doubt that this pride of race is the greatest barrier raised against missionaries and against the gospel in China. Even the humblest of Chinese men is not afflicted by an inferiority complex. But He who dealt with the Pharisee, Saul of Tarsus, has, we believe, also chosen for himself some rare jewels in southern Anhwei. It is only to work with our Lord in reaching His own that we came to China at all, not because we thought we would be able to convert this 'stiffnecked' race by our personalities! Neither did we choose the Chinese ways of thought and life; but that Christ, through a system of open and closed doors, sent us here. And, being here, it is by His grace alone that we stay—another thing entirely. Otherwise, who could endure such small annoyances.

"We traveled some two hundred miles in all. We had two men to carry our bedding, clothes, books and some food supplies, each man trotting along, balancing equal burdens at each end of a springy pole. About once an hour the procession would stop at a 'ten-li stop[1],' which might be the largest inn in a prosperous town, or maybe a mud hut from which a rude shelter spread over the path or highway, to the grat-

---

[1] ten-li, li is a Chinese unit of distance of about 3/8 mile. Ten-li would be nearly four miles.

itude of all travelers who stopped to smoke and rest and order a bowl of boiling water and tea leaves. Depending on the location and the time of day, we would soon move on again, or stop to eat what lunch we carried, or order something hot and savory. And always there would be an audience. At '*ten-li* stops' we often sold many gospels, the cheap, bright covers of which caught the eye of holiday crowds, and seized many opportunities to speak to the whole crowd or to fellow-travelers on the road about the true God and eternal life. At night, after we had settled down at an inn and had our supper we could always count on a crowd to listen to the words of life.

"Mr. and Mrs. Warren, who expect to go on furlough before the summer, have been living in Tsingteh for about a year, and it was they who rented the premises and fixed up the house for us. Mr. Warren met us before we came to the first group of Christians (called an out-station), and personally conducted us all over the field, with a week in Tsingteh itself. He and Mr. Stam had meetings in the evenings with the Christians, and in the daytime, accompanied by the Christians, would go into the villages. In the village squares and homes they held meetings, using scripture verses and posters to make clear to the eye what was not made clear to the ear by reason of the foreigner's accent and general lack of vocabulary. I had my opportunities with the women and children indoors. The general course of our trip might be likened to a rough baseball diamond—we went to Tsingteh (south of Suancheng) by a southwesterly route and returned from Tsingteh by a different route entirely, taking in an eastern point over the border into Chinkiang Province. When we say 'over the border' we mean it literally. The country became more and more mountainous, rice fields being entirely crowded out, leaving little for the local people to live on but corn—grown apparently for miles up on the precipitous slopes. We continued up the trail until we reached the pass, and then we went 'over the top,' and nearly tumbled down into the next province.

"In this mountainous country there is a cause for thanksgiving and continued prayer: an indigenous church, started with little outside help some thirty years ago, when the schoolteacher Cheng, bought some gospels, and later a whole Bible, from a traveling colporteur. Cheng and his son went to study this doctrine with the C.I.M. missionary of the district of Hweichow, and were baptized there. And since then the church in their own home has grown, and the son is a preacher helping one of our fellow-workers in another district of southern Anhwei. The group of Christians gathered around old Cheng, who loves to sing hymns, though it would be hard for other Christians to recognize either words or tunes. They sing their own Chinese tunes, and even their local speech is enough to frighten a poor missionary who was just starting to be able to understand and be understood by his fellowmen! But we feel that this work at Changhua is the most encouraging in our field, and, God willing, we would like to go "over the border" again, stay longer, and acquire enough of the difficult dialect to preach the Gospel in many, many villages and towns of those larger mountain valleys, and even in the smaller hamlets perched all around and among the mountain slopes."

The Stams stayed for one week with the Warrens
to obtain a general impression of the area before the
Warrens left on furlough. Betty saw the situation
quite clearly but was not discouraged by it. "There
is not much yet in the way of Christian life, but there
are one or two bright spots, and God is our hope anyway, or we would never attempt the work. . . ."

True to her usually cheerful, optimistic nature,
Betty emphasized the benefits of their new sphere of
service, commenting on the greater degree of comfort
in the houses, the more wholesome food and even
the standard of hygiene in the lodging-houses. Some
of the physical features of the landscape delighted
her poet's eye—stone bridges over clear-flowing
streams, the blue misty peaks beyond. They had the
advantage of a suitable church building all ready for
them with adequate living quarters in the back.

One great source of encouragement to them was
the out-station at Miaosheo. This meant a trek of
twelve miles across the mountains, but waiting to
welcome them after their exhaustive trip was Mrs.
Wang, who was the first Chinese to become a Christian in that area through listening to a C.I.M. director
preaching in the street some years previously. As she
heard the message of the Gospel, she ran to get her
husband and both became believers. "How could one
help believing," she said, "when told of such wonderful love?" From that time on, the Wangs were re-
nowned for their hospitality and they took the two
young newlyweds to their hearts.

Most of the other Christians were scattered out of
town, but they made an effort to come in for a service
and to meet the new missionaries. They would like

to have detained John and Betty longer, but on this first trip more ground had to be covered before they returned to Suancheng. Altogether they were away from base for twenty-four days, but the second half after Miaosheo proved much harder going. On the way there, John commented, "The walking was good," but in the second half, "The valleys were much narrower and passes higher to climb." Still there were compensations in the beautiful vistas down the trail and the good meeting they attended in the town of Chiki. John was counting on the help of Evangelist Lo when he had taken over the district, and the more he got to know him, the more thankful he became for such a dedicated and hard-working team member.

Another highlight of that missionary journey was meeting Brother Cheng in the small town of Chekiang. The story of his remarkable conversion was well known in those parts as Betty recounted in her magazine article. By the time John and Betty met him, he was already elderly, ". . . dressed in a foreign-style overcoat with great wide sleeves, a battered foreign hat and rimless glasses, his head thrown back, singing with all his might," according to their description. Now old Mr. Cheng had something to sing about and in meetings he would make a joyful, albeit unharmonious, noise to the Lord.

That book he had bought from the colporteur so many years ago comprised one of the gospels bound together with the Acts of the Apostles. But he didn't put it on a shelf to gather dust, he perused it very carefully from cover to cover, drinking in the contents. "This must be a message from the one true

God," he decided, "it has the ring of truth about it."
Next time the colporteur came along that way, Mr.
Cheng eagerly plied him with questions. "I gather it
is part of an even larger book. Could you let me have
the rest?"

So the colporteur hurried back with a complete
Bible. Mr. Cheng didn't just gloat over the treasures
contained in it for himself, he longed to share them
with others, and this he did in spite of ridicule and
persecution. As a result, his own son became pastor
over the little flock of converts. When the Stams arrived, eighteen church members were already gathered there and in the afternoon a baptismal service
was held. Betty and John were singularly impressed
by his story and the way he remained steadfast in the
face of opposition.

11

Gathering Clouds

C heered by the fellowship with Chinese Christians, the Stams set off once more on the last lap of their journey, which was probably the most hair-raising stage of the whole trip. The going was tough over high mountain passes, but even more difficult was negotiating the steep descent on the other side. Betty walked as far as she could and then accepted a lift in a chair, which gave John no peace of mind. He hovered anxiously near the worst precipices and even grabbed the poles himself when one of the bearers appeared likely to slip. After a twelve-hour stint they were exhausted, but relieved and happy to reach the bottom.

The next day was hardly luxurious but a vast improvement over the day before. They were able to relax comfortably on bedding spread over the deck of a boat taking them back to Suancheng. Though extremely grateful for safety and good health, they were a little overawed on their return by the large area for which they were responsible. Trekking for days was very different from looking at the extent of the region on a map—they had experienced for themselves the difficulties to be faced along the trail. Also, the population was spread over a large number of small villages rather than in the urban centers. Remember that in the 1930's, air travel was largely unavailable; even motor travel was difficult to obtain in rural China—so evangelization meant sheer hard work, on foot.

Now safely settled in their place of work, Betty knew the most recent missionary journey they'd made would be the last for her for some time to come—she very happily discovered she was expecting their first child. She shared the news eagerly with all the members of her family, and began collecting small clothing and items she would need for the little one. She and John discussed possible names for the baby.

Betty's parents had been anxiously concerned that perhaps she had overexerted herself in the early stages of her pregnancy, but when the baby arrived on September 11, 1934, all was well. A very healthy Helen Priscilla was born in the Methodist hospital in Wuhu near the great Yangtze River—in her parents eyes, everything that a baby should be.

John wrote that he was delightfully surprised at his daughter's appearance. Expecting a scrawny little red bundle, he was pleased to behold instead a "bonny baby." "She really is the cutest little thing . . . and would do for any baby show, as far as good looks are concerned. . . ." Betty thought Helen strikingly resembled her father John. Parental pride aside, she was reportedly a very contented child, sleeping soundly from 10 PM to 6 AM and most of the time from 6 AM to 10 PM. This happy, placid disposition was to stand baby Helen in good stead in the months to come. Betty did, however, admit in a letter to her family, "Last evening she kicked and howled so hard that I am afraid it was temper."

Granny Scott traveled all the way down from Tsinan to see her granddaughter when she was three weeks old and stayed to help Betty for a while. When her mother returned home, Betty felt a little unsure of herself, never having the experience before of caring for such a small charge. Was she too hot or too cold? Was she bundled enough, or too much? What was the cause of her crying? The age-old questions arose, and Betty had to deal with the questions and care alone, because while John would have loved to stay forever at the side of his new daughter, he needed to take advantage of the beautiful autumn weather while it lasted, and carry the Good News to those around them.

Soon he returned to the Tsingteh district, revisiting old contacts. He needed no persuasion to call on the Wang family again at Miaosheo and he experienced afresh the warmth of his first welcome. Unfortunately, the harvest was disastrous after a long hot summer with virtually no rain, making food scarce in the neighborhood. But Mrs. Wang, in spite of her lack of supplies, proved a skillful cook. John commented on her excellent meals, "She knows what the foreigner likes and what is good for him." She also kept her house—originally one of the well-known mansions which had depreciated in value after the T'ai-ping Rebellion—immaculate. Her hospitality was a veritable pleasure.

Mrs. Wang's husband was just as stalwart a Christian, walking twenty miles quite regularly for a service at Chiki. This involved a long weekend away from home and his secular work, but his service to the Lord was his priority, even if it lowered his business profits. One could never accuse the Wangs of making their appearance in the church a public show; the atmosphere in their home was an equal witness—the relationship between Mrs. Wang and her daughter-in-law being particularly caring. Bible studies held in their home were regular and fruit-bearing. John's association with the whole family was, needless to say, an exceptionally happy one. Leaving his young wife and new baby at home could not have been easy, but Mrs. Wang's motherly care and concern for his well-being during times of ministry compensated for his sacrifice—he was treated as her own son.

Obviously John had gained confidence in his use of the language for he wrote about his work in the open-air, chatting on the streets, giving away tracts and selling literature. He was thankful too for the company of Mr. E. A. Kohfield on the journey, while Betty and baby Helen remained in Wuhu, near the hospital. The two men discussed the possibility of a joint project in making a forward thrust with the gospel in their adjoining areas.

But a more serious threat engaged their immediate attention. A sense of uneasiness hung over the area due in part to the presence of many government troops. They had been drafted there to guard southern Anhwei from any inroads by Communist troops who had been uprooted from their bases in the neighboring province. The burden of this concentration of soldiers meant more mouths to feed, even though the crops had failed and food was scarce. Naturally, C.I.M. leaders were anxious to enlarge their sphere of influence, but not at the expense of the safety of their missionaries. So an exploratory visit was scheduled to evaluate local conditions by their own experience.

The men went to a good deal of trouble sizing up the situation, calling at Kinghsien, Miaosheo and finally Tsingteh, where John and Betty hoped to make their home. In an interview with Mr. Peng, the district magistrate, his first reaction was that John and Betty should delay their move for a while. There had been minor disturbances, mostly due to lack of adequate food supplies. Everyone was of the opinion, however, that it was extremely unlikely the Communists would advance any further. Indeed, later in their conversation with Mr. Peng, when he was challenged, he offered his protection to the Stams. "If there should be any trouble you can come to my yamen [his official residence]," and that seemed a very positive promise.

Still not completely satisfied with the situation, the men journeyed on to Tunki where they met with the same appraisal of circumstances. Mr. Lo, the district magistrate of this area, guaranteed their safety and again expressed his opinion that the Communists presented no immediate threat. In addition, Mr. Hanna, the C.I.M. superintendent in Anhwei, visited the area in person and arrived at the same conclusion as the native officials.

John found himself in a dilemma. He was no coward where the work of the Lord was being threatened, but now he had the added responsibility of the care of his wife and a very young baby. Would it be safe for them to move to Tsingteh? After prayerful consideration of all the evidence they had collected and the assurances they had been given by responsible local officials, he finally decided that it was time for them to take up their new sphere of service—"It appears right to advance," he wrote. It would be impossible to be one hundred percent sure of their personal safety, but then the same could be said of any area of missionary activity in the world. No one could blame him afterward for making a hasty, impulsive decision.

After some careful preparation, Betty was ready to leave the town where little Helen had been born. All their personal possessions had to be bundled up, ready to be transported by the slowest method available—a wheelbarrow—over the seventy miles to Tsingteh. It was a special joy for the proud parents to stop off at Suancheng en route to show their baby daughter to their Christian friends.

The believers took advantage of the Stams' visit to organize a short-term Bible school in town in which the missionaries could participate. But it was by no means run solely by foreign missionaries. John wrote appreciatively of the contributions made by two Chinese women Bible teachers. It was exciting to see how the Chinese church was producing its own leaders, pastors, teachers and preachers. C.I.M.'s policy was to encourage as many nationals as possible to take over gradually the running of the local churches.

Betty and John stayed with the Birches, and afterward Mrs. Birch wrote a full account of their visit. One very special service was held on Sunday when the Birches' baby son John and little Helen were dedicated to the Lord—a moving ceremony during which baby Helen behaved impeccably. Of course, the Birches and Stams were no strangers to each other, having shared a home in the beginning months of Betty and John's marriage. They had learned to love and appreciate one another through the close association. The Birches' little two-year-old David was strongly attached to Betty, as were many of the Chinese women and girls. She seemed to have a special rapport with them, perhaps due to her up-bringing in China and her understanding of their culture and customs.

John too had certainly won a place in the hearts of the Chinese with his genuine affection for them and interest in all that concerned them.

So John and Betty, together with Helen (Ai-lien in Chinese, meaning Love Link), set off again for Tsingteh, leaving their friends behind at Suancheng, with exceptionally happy memories of their visit. At her dedication, Mr. Weller had prayed that Helen Priscilla would take after her namesake, the biblical Priscilla, whose home was always open to minister to needy people. The Stams were full of faith that one day that prayer would be answered.

They did not reach their destination until the end of November, when the weather was beginning to turn very cold. Their living quarters were in a large, old Chinese house, and they were particularly grateful for the installation of two stoves. Their small staff—a cook and a general servant—had become faithful friends, so they had much to be thankful for: "We do praise the Lord for the privilege of being here," was John's comment in a letter written soon after their arrival. In spite of rumors of rice stealing in country districts, the general atmosphere was calm and free from foreboding fear. John felt satisfied with the step they had taken. Both felt they were in the place which the Lord had prepared for them—the culmination of many years of study and preparation.

John and Betty were careful not to impose their faith upon their neighbors, not wanting to produce "rice Christians"—those who would embrace their faith for material advantage. "To introduce Him to strangers . . . live so closely with and in Him that others may see that there really is such a person as Jesus, because some human being proves it by being like Him," was Betty's desire expressed in a letter to a young brother while she was still at college.

12

The Storm Breaks

Earlier in Betty's life, she had written her testimony from which she never deviated. At one point in time, it was uncertain whether doctors would pass her as fit for service in China, but she had thought through her commitment in full in spite of possible obstacles.

"People have always expected me, as the daughter of missionaries in China, to return there someday—but that is not why I am planning to be a foreign missionary. I was born in China, and learned from childhood to love the East, with its antique culture, its picturesqueness, its calm, happy-go-lucky people—but that is not why I am going to return, either. My own home is over there, and the two people I love most in the world—but even that is not what makes a missionary, and keeps her on the field, and I would never dare set myself up, even as an embryonic one, if something had not revolutionized my whole life first, and given me my first true call to mission work . . .

"I am willing, of course, to go anywhere He wants me to go (if He will only show me the way clearly): but naturally my thoughts swing back with renewed interest to China, my beloved 'native land,' where I have personal acquaintance with the language and the need. That firsthand knowledge of conditions constitutes, I believe, my second big reason for returning to the foreign field . . .

"And finally, there is a third reason why I am hoping to return to the foreign field, and that is—I want something really worthwhile to live for. Like most young people, I want to invest this one life of mine as wisely as possible, in the place that yields richest profits to the world and me. This may not be in China; it may be in India or Africa, or our own squalid slums in New York. But, wherever it is, I want it to be God's choice for me and not my own. There must be no self-interest at all, or I do not believe God can reveal His will clearly. Certainly Paul never saw his vision of the man from Macedonia by looking in his own mirror. I know very well that I can never realize the richest, most satisfying, life Christ meant for me, if I am not giving my own life unselfishly for others. Christ said: 'He that would find his life shall lose it,' and proved the truth of this divine paradox at Calvary. I want Him to lead, and His Spirit to fill me. And then, only then, will I feel that my life is justifying its existence and realizing the maturity in Him that Christ meant for all men, in all parts of the world."

Although a few years had passed since then, Betty's outlook had not changed in spite of some of the rigors of missionary life. Fortunately, her youthful sense of humor helped when she was confronted with flies, rats and a complete lack of privacy!

December 5 was the last full day they spent together as a family in their home in Tsingteh. No premonition of sudden violent disruption troubled them. Betty bathed, fed and played with little Helen as usual. She supervised her two faithful servants while they prepared the meals and cleaned the house, and made the lists for shopping in the local market for fresh food supplies. Perhaps to those not accustomed to the culture in China fifty years ago, two servants in the home may seem redundant. But there were no labor-saving devices, everything needing to be done by hand or made from scratch. For the peasant women, jobs in the homes of foreigners were especially coveted because of the better food and living conditions. In the case of the servants in the home of the Stams, it was far more than these privileges that endeared them to the young family—there was a strong, warm bond among them.

Of course once little Helen had grown, Betty would have relied on the servants' help even more, while she spent more time in language study and visiting the Chinese women in their homes. Missionary work for the women could really only be done adequately with the help of servants in the home. At that point in time Helen was only three months old, and Betty was devoted to spending all her time in the care of the child.

While the normal domestic routine was carried on, John was writing to friends in his hometown of Paterson. Almost prophetically he wrote, "Things are always happening otherwise than one expects . . .

The Lord helps us to be quite satisfied, whatever he sends our way this day." He mentioned, too, the rigid scrutiny to which all missionaries were subjected. He felt the need to be constantly on guard so that none of his words or actions would prove contrary to his beliefs—a difficult standard for both of them to maintain.

Almost as if he had been forewarned, John had also written an Easter article for a student magazine on the theme of "Except a corn of wheat fall into the ground and die, it abideth alone: but if it die, it bringeth forth much fruit" (John 12:24–28). These were the Lord's own words before His supreme hour of trial. John commented, too, on the Lord's poignant statement, "Now is my soul troubled Father, save me from this hour: but for this cause came I unto this hour." So, in theory, John had already accepted the Lord's claim on his life under any circumstances. All that remained was to discover whether his behavior would match his convictions under intense pressure.

Within hours they were put to the test. On December 6, the city of Tsingteh was dramatically and unexpectedly captured by the Red forces. With a detailed knowledge of the local terrain, they traversed the mountains by little-known tracks and came in behind the government forces which lay sixty miles in a southerly direction. Their coup took everyone by surprise. Tsingteh was still one of the old Chinese walled cities, but the foremost troops crept up under cover of darkness and scaled the walls preparatory to flinging open the huge, heavy city gates. Betty was giving baby Helen her early morning bath when the first messenger came trembling into the house with news of the impending invasion. Soon he was followed by others, breathless and fearful in the rush, but it was already too late to heed the warning and plan an effectual escape.

Betty and John were already well-liked and respected in the city despite their comparatively short residence there. People knew that they, as foreigners, would be particularly vulnerable in the face of any impending uprising. The old attitude of the Chinese to foreigners died hard. The Boxer Rebellion was still fresh in the minds of some of the people, and in the long centuries of isolation the Western nations had bred a certain amount of suspicion against them. So those who came to warn the Stams knew of the danger, and the very real chance of their being taken captive and being made a scapegoat for any possible trouble in the area, whatever the cause.

Panic was already rife in the streets. The district magistrate, after putting up a token show of resistance, had fled while the escape routes were still open. Anyone with money tried to obtain means of transport to escape the Red troops. Chairs and coolies were in great demand, but the availability of both became scarce very quickly; there simply weren't enough for everyone at once. To their dismay and terror, citizens heard the sounds of firing on the streets and knew beyond any doubt that the plunder of the city by enemy forces had already begun. All avenues of escape were sealed.

In contrast to the uproar outside, John and Betty did the only reasonable thing to them under the circumstances—they knelt to pray together with their women servants. They were only human in their fear for their lives and that of their baby, but they knew where to turn in such a crisis. In the past they had proved the power of prayer and knew that the Lord would stand by them in their hour of need. The action served to compose the thoughts and minds of all present.

Determined to "turn the other cheek," both perhaps to win them over by a friendly manner and also to show a Christian attitude toward their would-be enemies, John interviewed the leaders first of all, trying to comply with their demands for household goods, personal possessions and above all, money. Betty, with her usual courtesy, offered them the tea and cakes she had prepared; but the crisis was not to be averted as easily as that. Whether their hearts were inwardly touched by this sincere display of friendliness and hospitality, no one will ever know. At least they showed no outward sign of a change of attitude and ended the confrontation by binding John securely and taking him off to the Communist headquarters.

There had been no time to prepare for such an outrage as this. When, in all good faith, after making exhaustive enquiries about the political situation, John and the C.I.M. leaders had decided the way was open to them in that province, the Stams had taken up residence in Tsingteh with the utmost confidence that they would live there in safety. Yet, after only a few short weeks, they suddenly found themselves in the hands of the Communists. As soon as John had been dragged away, Betty's thoughts turned to supplies for herself and the baby. What would they need if a similar fate met them? In spite of her firm faith,

how she must have felt anxious for her husband—
How long would he be kept in captivity and would
he be roughly treated?

A commotion outside made her hope wildly that
he had been quickly returned with his papers in order
but it was not to be so. Instead, the soldiers had come
back, this time to arrest Betty and the baby. In vain
the cook and the maid pleaded with the soldiers to
be allowed to accompany them. "If you move in their
direction, we will shoot you immediately," was their
stern, uncompromising reply.

With her characteristic thoughtfulness for other
people, Betty tried to calm their fears. Softly she
whispered in their ears, "It might turn out for the best
if you stay here after all. We understand; we realize
you're not letting us down; there is no alternative.
Besides, just suppose anything happened to John and
myself—you could care for the baby."

She was given no more time to say goodbye, but
was brusquely taken off by the soldiers to join her
husband—satisfied that she had been able to murmur
a last crucial message to the servants. She had done
all she could; now she could only leave matters in
the hands of the Lord. For the next few hours John
and Betty were able to comfort each other and in spite
of finding themselves in a desperate situation, eye-
witnesses attested that they showed no outward signs
of fear.

Remarkably, when John was released for a short
while and allowed to return to their home, which had
been looted, he with typical unselfishness sought to
comfort the servants who had remained. The main
objective of the visit was to secure more food and

clothing for the baby, should their imprisonment stretch out over a long period. Betty had been snatched away before having time to make adequate preparations, so they lacked many basic necessities. Of course he was closely guarded by a contingent of soldiers, but that did not inhibit him from speaking out fearlessly to the weeping women. Their distress was unbounded by the Stams' arrest and the thorough ransacking of the home by the Communist forces.

"Don't be afraid," he said to one servant who was still in a state of shock and discomfort. "God is on the throne. These little things are immaterial—our Heavenly Father knows all about them. Your best plan is to go and sleep with old Mis-hi tonight, and the cook will look after you."

13

Captivity

December 6, 1934

China Inland Mission
Shanghai
Tsingteh, An.

Dear Brethren,

My wife, baby and myself are today in the hands of the Communists, in the city of Tsingteh. Their demand is twenty thousand dollars for our release.

All our possessions and supplies are in their hands, but we praise God for peace in our hearts and a meal tonight. God grant you wisdom in what you do, and us fortitude, courage and peace of heart. He is able—and a wonderful Friend in such a time.

Things happened so quickly this AM. They were in the city just a few hours after the ever-persistent rumors really became alarming, so that we could not prepare to leave in time. We were just too late.

The Lord bless and guide you, and as for us, may God be glorified whether by life or by death.

In Him,
John C. Stam

How John managed to scribble this short letter in such difficult conditions, with bloodshed and looting all around, seems incredible. It is remarkable, too, how he managed to get this note into the hands of the right people so it reached its destination. Poignant in its tense brevity, it nevertheless gives an insight into what they were passing through. John could have begged the staff at C.I.M. headquarters to make every attempt to collect together what was then a very large sum demanded for their ransom. He put them under no such obligation, being unwilling to place them in any financial quandary when funds were always difficult.

He could have bemoaned the loss of almost all their worldly possessions, but he made only a passing reference to the fact. Probably the most outstanding comment was, ". . . we praise God for peace in our hearts and a meal tonight."

It is reminiscent of Paul and Silas singing praises to God at midnight in the jail at Philippi after they had been beaten and put in the stocks (Acts 16). Wasn't it Paul who also said, "In everything give thanks." (Phil. 4:6)?

There is a supernatural calm running through this letter—only a man closely in touch with God could have penned such a note. Notice that it did not read like a statement written to impress people, but a straightforward honest declaration of the facts. Betty must have shared his composure because he writes in the plural, "we praise God for peace in our hearts." He did not appear unduly optimistic—or pessimistic about the outcome, " ... may God be glorified whether by life or by death" was his closing sentence. Obviously, they acknowledged the possibility of losing their lives before the episode was over; it was by no means certain that they would be released unharmed.

This letter was published both in the February and March editions of *China's Millions* and remains as a precious memoir in the Mission's archives. Only one other note, shorter than the first, came from John's hand after that.

It was no token force that had taken possession of the district. Beginning with an army of two thousand Communists, it soon swelled to six thousand and was in complete control, having dealt with all effective opposition. The poor peasants were ill-equipped to suffer any more hardships. Already reduced to semi-famine conditions by the failure of their harvests, they had to suffer the agony of seeing their meager resources being snatched away before their eyes. That in itself was sufficient reason to despair, but by no means the worst evil they would have to suffer. Many friends, relatives and neighbors were brutally slaughtered by the troops, summarily executed without any justification. They were given no chance to plead their cause but murdered on the spot before any investigation of their so-called "crimes" could be carried out. Anarchy reigned.

Some, who were spared an immediate execution, were seized and carried away as captives when the

Red troops evacuated Tsingteh the next morning, the majority of them innocent victims of a civil war neither caused nor wanted by them. The army commanders had resolved to head for Miaosheo next, the little town which lay just about twelve miles across the mountains. John and Betty were no doubt uninformed of their destination—it being highly unlikely that the Communists would have revealed their plans to foreign, white missionaries. But when they realized along the trail in which direction they were heading, they must have felt a pang of regret for their Christian friends there, being unwilling to implicate them in their own sorry plight.

John and Betty both treasured the happy memories of their former visits there with Mr. and Mrs. Wang. Now they must have feared it would distress their kind, caring Christian friends to see them in captivity, and perhaps even cause some difficulty for them when it was seen that the Chinese converts had enjoyed a previous association with the missionaries. But obviously there was no way to warn the Wangs or any other church members of their impending arrival.

Mercifully, John must have had his bonds released sufficiently to carry baby Helen. She must have seemed a very precious and welcome burden, in spite of the weary trek of twelve miles, especially when it had appeared earlier that she may be killed before they even set out from Tsingteh—no doubt a ploy to torture the minds of the parents. The Reds were ruthless men who would stop at nothing to gain their own ends. Life was extremely cheap in their hands.

Oddly enough, the baby was saved by a casual remark while the men were discussing whether to kill Helen on the spot. "Why bother to kill her?" queried one of the soldiers. "She's bound to die anyway— we can save ourselves the trouble." And so her life was spared; God had other plans in mind for that little one. Betty was allowed to ride on horseback at least part of the way, and both the parents managed to smile at a few folks who watched them passing along the way. In their quiet way, they managed to convey an inner sense of peace and well-being that completely belied the nightmare through which they were passing.

On their arrival in the village, their first instinct must have been to seek out their friends the Wangs, but utter chaos predominated. A few fortunate citizens had already fled, being forewarned of the Communists' intentions. Houses were looted and family treasures stolen or thrown out, broken and smashed on the streets outside. Neither possessions nor human lives were held sacred by the Red forces. They destroyed whom or what they willed. John and Betty were marched under guard to the post office, where they were only too glad to be spared the sight of all the pillage and murder around them.

The postmaster at least recognized the prisoners, dirty and disheveled as they now appeared after their cruel treatment and long, forced march. It was true that he had only seen Betty once before, but John had spent some time there, and foreigners being quite a rare sight in those regions, one was not likely to forget them. "Where are you going?" he asked, astonished by their plight but unable to help. "We do not know where *they* are going," was John's characteristically simple reply, "but we are going to heaven." There was no need for further explanation. The kindly man offered them some fruit; it was all he dared to do on their behalf. Betty thankfully accepted some. It had been some hours since the last meal in Tsingteh, and they had since endured a strenuous journey. Additionally, Betty was still nursing the baby and was anxious to keep up her milk supply as long as possible, it being Helen's only form of nourishment. There was no guarantee when they might be given food again, if at all.

John did not stop to eat, having more pressing business to attend to. Seizing the opportunity, he wrote the following letter, again to Shanghai, to fill in the mission leaders with the latest details to keep them aware of the prevailing circumstances. Again, it contained no frenzied plea for release at all costs, no insistence that missionary funds should be diverted for that purpose. "God give you wisdom in what you do," was his sincere prayer.

December 7, 1934

China Inland Mission
Miaosheo, An.

Dear Brethren,

We are in the hands of the Communists here, being taken from Tsingteh when they passed through yesterday. I tried to persuade them to let my wife and baby go back from Tsingteh with a letter to you, but they wouldn't let her, and so we both made the trip to Miaosheo today, my wife traveling part of the way on a horse.

They want $20,000 before they will free us, which we have told them we are sure will not be paid. Famine relief money and our personal money and effects are all in their hands. God give you wisdom in what you do and give us grace and fortitude. He is able.

Yours in Him,
John C. Stam

When this letter was reprinted in the March 1935 issue of *China's Millions*, the editor added beneath John's signature, the following verse from a hymn.

For all the saints who from their labors rest,
Who Thee by faith before the world confessed,
Thy Name, Oh Jesus, be for ever blessed.
Alleluia.

Obviously, John wasn't convinced that his first letter had gotten through, so he repeated the first piece of information that they had been taken captive by the Communists in Tsingteh. There was no hint of the pressure they were under revealed in his writing. He could have been forgiven if he had begged the Mission at least to spare no cost in rescuing Betty and the baby. But he and Betty were unified in thought and purpose. They were both in a crisis situation together with God's hand over them for good. It would be God who had the last word and not the Red army officers. God would only allow them to be killed if it was in His best plan and purpose for them.

There was no time or opportunity to send messages to relatives or close friends, so these two missives contain all the information that remains. After carrying out certain duties in town, the Communists had time to concentrate on their white prisoners once more. Their fate was no doubt already decided, but they were moved from the post office to the home of a wealthy man who had fled the town. There they were taken to a room just off an inner courtyard with a number of soldiers to guard them. To further intimidate them, they bound John to the frame of a heavy bed with thick ropes, even though it would have been virtually impossible to escape with so many soldiers surrounding them. To Betty they were more merciful, allowing her to be free to attend to the baby, while John was left almost unable to shift his position, throughout the long hours of that December night of uncomfortably low temperatures.

14

The Last Missionary Journey

No record exists of the last few hours they spent together. Betty would doubtless have shared her time between settling the baby down after a feeding and trying to alleviate John's cramped agony. While the baby slept, they would have had time to pray and talk together, perhaps surmise about the baby's future.

It seemed extremely unlikely that they would share that future with her, but the tiny life had already been dedicated to the Lord and they were content to leave her in His hands rather than those of any human. They must have wondered who would come to her rescue when they were snatched from her, but their faith sustained them and they did all they could for her with their scant resources.

Dawn broke at last. The guards marched in and bound the couple with ropes. Taking a last glance at baby Helen, they were hustled out of the room and forced to walk painfully along the street with their hands tied behind them. Spectators, many of whom knew them, were amazed at their calmness under such frightful conditions.

The Red soldiers shouted insulting remarks at the prisoners and called the townspeople to come and witness the execution.

Leaving the main street, they were taken to a clump of pine trees on a hill a short distance from the town. Communist agitators addressed the crowd, trying to force their political arguments upon them; to brainwash them into agreeing with the murder of these two innocent people, only twenty-seven and twenty-eight years old. No one in the crowd dared contradict the captors, although all knew only too well that John and Betty had never been involved in politics and had no connection with the general state of unrest throughout the district.

Finally, a Christian medical worker had the courage to step out and on his knees beg that mercy be shown to his two friends. Pushed to one side, he carried on pleading for their lives until he also was bound and taken off when the Communists discovered that he too was a Christian.

John's last act of concern was to plea for mercy for this brother who had risked everything to beg for their lives to be spared. The only reply was a curt command to kneel, and with one stroke his head was severed. People who caught a glimpse of his face, afterward spoke of seeing a genuine expression of joy. Betty trembled momentarily and fell on her knees also, her hands still bound behind her back. Another flash of a sword and her body sank lifeless next to her husband's.

To everyone in the town, it must have seemed like the end of a long, bittersweet story. One by one, the townsfolk slunk back inside their houses, released from the horrible scene they had just witnessed. Even when darkness fell, nobody dared to venture out, even though some were aware of the whereabouts of baby Helen. The Reds had withdrawn about three miles away and could pounce again at any time. Meanwhile spies remained in the area, so the bodies were left where they fell, no attempt being made to remove them for burial. Far into the night, people discussed the tragedy in whispers while a tiny baby lay crying alone in the abandoned house. Help was to come from an unexpected quarter. God is never taken by surprise, and His plan was in effect for the child.

Refugees had been hiding from the Communists in the hills above the town, almost without food and shelter. Among them was Evangelist Lo and his wife who had originally planned to join the Stams in Miaosheo. Because of the unstable political situation they were late in arriving to take up their duties— which turned out for the best, since they would certainly have been killed or taken prisoner had they already occupied the Mission premises. Kind Mrs. Wang, hospitable as ever, had welcomed them into her home, but trouble struck in the night and the women were forced to flee to the mountains, leaving Mr. Lo and Mrs. Wang's son to try to defend their property and their lives.

Soon their own lives were in jeopardy when the

Communists sought them out as head men of the town. Wang managed to escape but Lo faced the soldiers, seeing no reason to run, since he held no official position. But he was nonetheless taken prisoner. Then Chang, the Christian pharmacist who forfeited his life on the next day pleading for Betty and John, spoke up for Evangelist Lo. "This man doesn't even live here, he travels around giving away literature and helping to cure diseases. I know him—I can vouch for him."

In this case the pleading paid off, and Mr. Lo was freed. He slipped away quietly trying to blend unobtrusively into the background. Then he made his way back to the other refugees. Although free, little comfort remained for them. Afraid to make a fire in case their presence was detected, they ate the raw vegetation around them and huddled together for warmth. They must have had some contact with the townspeople because word reached them that a foreigner was being held by the Reds. Later the news was that two were held—a husband and wife who had later been executed. The details left them in little doubt as to the identity of the victims.

Sunday, December 9, gave them a short breathing space. From their vantage point, the refugees witnessed skirmishes between government troops and Communists who had been drawn away from the town in pursuit of their enemies. The Wangs, together with Mr. and Mrs. Lo and their small son, suffering from malnutrition and exposure, took the opportunity to creep back quietly into the town. Making discreet enquiries, Lo was unable to make some headway. His friend Chang was strangely nowhere to be found, and people who obviously knew something kept their lips sealed for fear of recrimination. One old lady with more courage than the others plucked his sleeve and whispered in his ear, "There's a foreign baby alive up there," but refused to say more.

Lo followed the direction in which she pointed and entered the desolate, empty house. At first there was no trace of a baby in room after room, but plenty of evidence that the rebel army had occupied the place. Heaps of filth and shattered household goods were strewn over the floors. Suddenly a tiny cry broke the silence. Lo hurried in the direction of the sound and had the joy of taking little Helen into his arms, apparently undaunted by her thirty-hour fast. He could hardly believe his senses. Betty had zipped her up inside a warm sleeping bag and left her on a bed—the safest possible place.

Not wanting to spend much time in the danger-fraught area he hurried with her up the hill. There the full horror of the tragedy finally struck him when he came across the two decapitated bodies lying where they had fallen in pools of their own blood. Fearful that the Reds would return at any moment, he hurried back to the Wangs with the baby and left her with his wife.

Later the brave little party, including Mrs. Wang and her son, retrieved the bodies, wrapped them in white cotton cloth, and placed them lovingly in wooden coffins.

When it seemed the Reds were out of the area, other people came out onto the streets, openly expressing their sorrow at the deaths of Betty and John. Lo seized the opportunity to address them. "Don't grieve for them—they are already with their Father in Heaven. They came many thousands of miles to preach the Gospel to you. You mustn't forget their words. Repent and believe the message.''

Still feeling the time was short to smuggle Helen out of the district, Lo did not take the time for a burial service. Then it was discovered that someone had stolen what little money and few possessions they owned from the Wang's house. He was faced with the problem of transporting a foreign, white baby and his own desperately ill little boy across one hundred miles of mountainous terrain riddled with Communist soldiers. It looked like an impossible task.

At this time, the forethought with which Betty Stam prepared to leave her tiny child forever, was discovered. Her own anguish put aside, she had tucked inside the sleeping bag several clean diapers, a fresh nightgown and two five-dollar bills! The money provided the very miracle the Lo's so urgently needed. Without it, the children could not have been whisked to safety.

Leaving Miaosheo with the utmost secrecy, Mr. and Mrs. Lo were able to hire a man to carry a yoke over his shoulders from which were suspended two large rice baskets. These contained the two little ones, discreetly hidden from sight. Baby Helen slept a good deal of the way. At their frequent stops, several young Chinese mothers took turns nursing her, soothing and satisfying her needs for the next stage of the journey. The Lo's small son revived after many hours of unconsciousness and, much to his parents' delight, eventually made a complete recovery.

Fortunately, Mrs. Lo had also been a patient at the

Wuhu Methodist Hospital for her baby's birth. She had received a baby bottle there, and being familiar with the foreign method of feeding babies, she bought a tin of Lactogen formula in Kingshsien. This ensured the baby's regular feedings for the rest of the trip. Few Chinese women in the whole of the country would have had this knowledge in the 1930's, but to the anxious Lo's, it seemed as though God had specially trained and prepared them to be able to give little Helen the routine to which she was accustomed.

Meanwhile, anxiety grew among those of the Mission as the news of the Stams' imprisonment spread, but their fate remained uncertain. Much prayer was made for them, everyone knowing that the Communists could be fanatically cruel and liable to stop at nothing if it suited their purposes.

A week after John's last appeal, Mr. Birch heard a knock on his door. His wife was away in Wuhu with the children, and he rose to answer it. At first he was unable to recognize the weary woman standing before him in torn and muddy garments, but closer scrutiny revealed that it was Mrs. Lo.

"This is all we have left," she said, unable to hold back her tears. At first Mr. Birch assumed that her husband had been killed by the Communists and the little child was her own baby son. But when Mrs. Lo extended the bundle as if offering it to Mr. Birch, he took the child and loosened the shawl around her. To his utter amazement, he was looking into the little face of baby Helen.

Then Mr. Lo, who had not yet appeared in the doorway, came in and filled in the details of tragedy. Mr. Birch was overwhelmed with grief at hearing of the deaths of John and Betty, but at the same time overjoyed at the miracle that little Helen's life was spared.

Helen Priscilla was soon taken to Wuhu hospital for an examination and was found to be perfectly healthy. She still retained her placid nature and charmed everyone with her smiling and cooing. To her grandparents, her safekeeping was a most wonderful and miraculous gift:

"Everything about her deliverance tells of God's love and power. And we know that if He could bring a tiny, helpless infant, not three months old, through such dangers in perfect safety, He could no less surely have saved the lives of her precious parents, had that been in His divine plan for them."

An article from *The Prairie Overcomer* published some months afterward, revealed the depth of Betty's dedication to Christ and His cause, and her mother's insight into her experience:

"Lord, I give up my own purposes and plans, all my own desires and hopes and ambitions (whether they be fleshly or soulish) and accept Thy will for my life. I give myself, my life, my all utterly to Thee, to be Thine forever. I hand over to Thy keeping all of my friendships; all the people whom I love are to take a second place in my heart. Fill me and seal me with Thy Holy Spirit. Work out Thy whole will in my life, at any cost, now and forever. To me to live is Christ. Amen!"

Nine years after making this statement, on December 8, 1934, Betty Scott Stam and her husband calmly and bravely laid down their lives for Christ when they were martyred by Chinese Communists.

As Mrs. Scott further spoke of lessons of trust and faithfulness from the lives of John and Betty, she said that Betty's victory over the power of the enemy in that dark hour in 1934 had actually been won at Keswick in 1925. Betty was victor in the crisis because years before, she had utterly yielded herself to the Lord Jesus Christ and trusted Him to be her victor."

John's father, Peter, wrote to friends who had sent letters of sympathy:

"Our dear children, John and Betty, have gone to be with the Lord. They loved Him. They served Him and now they are with Him. What could be more glorious? As for those of us who have been left behind, we are reminded by a telegram from one of John's former schoolmates, 'Remember, you gave John to God, not to China.' Our hearts, though bowed for a little while with sadness, answered, 'Amen' . . .

"We are earnestly praying that it will all be for God's glory and the salvation of souls. How glad we shall be if through this dreadful experience many souls shall be won for the Lord Jesus . . .

"We were honored by having sons and daughters minister for our Lord among the heathen, but we are more signally honored that two of them have received the martyr's crown.

"We are sure that our dear brother and sister, Doctor and Mrs. C. E. Scott both join us in saying, 'The Lord gave, and the Lord hath taken away; blessed be the name of the Lord.' "

Peter Stam did not have to wait long for an answer to his fervent prayers. Seven hundred students stood up in the memorial service held in the Moody Bible Institute to consecrate their lives to missionary work in whatever part of the world God might appoint them.

Letters began to pour in from all over the world to Dr. and Mrs. Scott; also gifts to little Helen Priscilla. Betty's own Wilson College took over the financial care of the baby; calling her "The College Baby" and covering the whole of the costs of her higher education. The students also made an on-the-spot collection and sent out to China a hundred dollars for her immediate needs.

"John and Betty had heavenly perspective," wrote Dr. Scott. "Given that, all other things fall into their proper proportions."

The February and March issues of *China's Millions* added further comment to the tragedy, although no more information about the sequence of events.

"We think of martyrs, usually, as men and women of other days, remote from our own time and knowledge. That two young missionaries, therefore, known to many on this continent and having gone out from our midst so recently that their farewell messages are still fresh in our minds, should be called upon, in their service for Christ, to submit to sudden and brutal death—this amazes us. And yet the grace and strength of the Lord was theirs in the hour of supreme trial . . .

"John Stam, in writing to his father some time before, and mentioning the prevailing dangers, had enclosed verses which, though written by another, he said expressed his own feelings.

AFRAID?

Afraid? Of what?

To feel the spirit's glad release?
To pass from pain to perfect peace,
The strife and strain of life to cease?
Afraid—of that?

Afraid? Of what?
Afraid to see the Savior's face,
To hear His welcome, and to trace
The glory gleam from wounds of grace?
Afraid—of that?

Afraid? Of what?
A flash—a crash—a pierced heart;
Darkness—Light—O Heaven's art!
A wound of His a counterpart!
Afraid?—of that?

Afraid? Of what?
To do by death what life could not—
Baptize with blood a stony plot,
Till souls shall blossom from the spot?
Afraid?—of that?

"Mrs. Stam was the daughter of Dr. and Mrs. Charles Ernest Scott, well-known in this country and laboring in China under the American Presbyterian Mission . . . When the first telegram reached Dr. Scott from C.I.M. headquarters at Shanghai, reporting the rumor of Mr. and Mrs. Stam having been captured by Communists, he wrote in a letter to Mr. Stam's parents in America: 'Please pray that, if still on earth, Betty and John and little Helen Priscilla may soon be released, provided this is God's will for them . . . John and Betty are radiant with love for Jesus Christ, and passionate to make Him known to those who apart from them will never hear the Good News . . . No matter how much they may be tortured, or whatever happens to them, they will not deny their Lord but will be good soldiers of Jesus Christ.'

"Upon learning later that his dear daughter and son-in-law had been slain, Dr. Scott said prophetically: 'They have not died in vain ... If we could hear our beloved children speak, we know from their convictions that they would praise God because He counted them worthy to suffer for the sake of Christ.' Truly, the Lord must have a high and holy purpose in permitting this sacrifice, and we believe that to many a God-devoted heart the challenge will come: 'Who follows in their train?' "

The article went on to relate the number of messages of sympathy which had been received, also offers of help for the little baby, even suggestions of adoption by Christian families.

"One lady candidate, who was first influenced toward China by Betty Scott (Mrs. Stam) when they were students together at Wilson College, writes, 'I do not fear death, but would be happy to die in China or here for Christ's cause. The chief desire would be that my death should be a means of leading precious souls to Christ. Being human, I naturally dread suffering and distress of body, and abuse at the hands of wicked men, but I really believe that I have faced all these possibilities and counted the cost. This tragic and terrible happening does not frighten me but rather makes me regird myself with the armor of God.'

"It has been a long time since any event connected with the mission fields has made so wide and profound an impression in this country. We believe that John and Betty Stam may by their death have spoken even more loudly than by their brief lives of devoted service. Let no one call this ending of their earthly career a tragedy, for in reality it is a triumph. It recalls to mind the old seal of the noble Moravian Brotherhood consisting of a lamb upon a crimson background, together with a cross of resurrection and a banner of victory. Underneath all was the motto in Latin which, translated into English, reads: OUR LAMB HAS CONQUERED; LET US FOLLOW HIM. John and Betty Stam were true followers of the Lamb—in life, and even unto death. Again the challenge comes: 'Who follows in their train?' ''

Epilogue

STAND STILL AND SEE

A poem by Elisabeth Scott (Mrs J.C. Stam), published in the *Sunday School Times*.

> I'm standing, Lord.
> There is a mist that blinds my sight.
> Sharp jagged rocks, front, left, and right.
> Hover, dim, gigantic in the night.
> Where is the way?
>
> I'm standing, Lord.
> The black rock hems me in behind
> Above my head a moaning wind
> Chills and oppresses heart and mind.
> I am afraid!
>
> I'm standing, Lord.
> The rock is hard beneath my feet.
> I nearly slipped Lord on the sleet.
> So weary, Lord and where a seat?
> Still must I stand?

He answered me, and on His face
A look ineffable of grace,
Of perfect, understanding love,
Which all my murmuring did remove.

I'm standing, Lord.
Since Thou hast spoken, Lord I see
Thou hast beset; these rocks are Thee;
And since Thy love encloses me,
    I stand and sing.

In the next issue of *China's Millions*, dated March 1935, Mr. G.A. Birch paid a tribute to his martyred colleague. He was well qualified to do that, as you remember early on in their married life the Stams had shared a home with the Birches. It could not have been an easy situation for newlyweds—denied the total privacy they would probably have preferred. Even under the stress of studying for exams a happy and cordial relationship existed between them all. Mr. Birch was also the first white missionary to see and hold Helen Priscilla after her parents' death, and made immediate arrangements for her future care. The following is his tribute:

"Our dear friends and fellow-workers John and Betty Stam have passed to their glorious reward. We cherish their memory and realize deeply the privilege that was ours of having them in our home for a season. How clearly I remember the day Mr. Stam arrived. I met him at the launch. He was six feet two, every inch a man. His hearty grip and bright smile clinched our friendship at once. As we proceeded in the sampan, [a small boat used in the Far East] the conversation at once turned to the things of God, for

John lived with God and loved to talk of those things which filled his heart.

"On our first itineration together we had to walk all one day in the rain and mud, but John's ardor was in no way dampened. That trip was a great blessing to me for he was mighty in the Scriptures, full of zeal to make CHRIST known, and full of love to the lost souls about him. Of course he did not have much language then, but he used what he had and quickly acquired more. John was very quick to see the hand of God in everything. One day he had contracted a heavy cold and was tired from a long walk. We felt the need of some green vegetables but there seemed no possibility of getting any. We stopped to preach the gospel in all small villages, and without a word from us the woman at the door of whose tea shop we were preaching, and who knew our Chinese companion, prepared a good meal for us. There were six or eight different kinds of vegetable, most of them very nicely salted for they could not be bought fresh. What a surprise! John said, 'Can GOD prepare a table in the wilderness?' He often used to say, 'My heavenly Father knows.' And once, when speaking of difficulties he quoted the Lord's words, 'For this cause came I unto this hour.' Truly he followed in his Lord's footsteps even unto death, and I know that he rejoiced in the fact that GOD was guiding and that CHRIST was glorified.

"During the first summer that Mr. Stam was in China he was alone with the Chinese brethren at Suancheng for two months. He made marvelous progress in the language, and got very close to the Chinese. He carried on regular services for children, and one Sunday even led the main service, preaching a sermon in Chinese. This when he had not been one year in China.

"In the fall of 1933, after one year in China, Mr. Stam went up to Tsinan and returned with his bride. They were ideally happy. A text from God's Word flashes to my mind: 'They were lovely and pleasant in their lives and in their death they were not divided.' Betty Stam was a savor of CHRIST wherever she was. Women and children loved to visit her and always received a welcome which did them good.

"In the early spring of this year, Rev. R. Graham, Jr., a very fluent Chinese speaker and powerful evangelist, led our church conference at Suancheng. John Stam was invited to be a leader in the conference at Kinghsien held later, and he was asked to give the messages which Mr. Graham had given at Suancheng with such blessing. This was no small accomplishment for a man who had been in China only sixteen months, but John did it, speaking twice daily for three or four days. This is a sample of the wholehearted way in which he threw himself into his work, and of the power of God which rested upon him.

"A little later John and Betty Stam visited Miaosheo spending a weekend there and witnessing for CHRIST in the place where they were later martyred. John visited this place again with Mr. Kohfield in October, and though they only spent one night in the town, yet they met together with the Christians in Bible study and prayer, and also found time to distribute tracts on the street and to speak to a number of individuals of the things of God. On November 23, our dear friends left us and moved to their new

work at Tsingteh, of which Miaosheo is an out-
station. Two weeks later they were taken captive to
Miaosheo, there to witness in a new way. Much work
has been expanded in the work of the Gospel at
Miaosheo, and in former years there were many believers. Some are dead, some have moved away,
many have grown cold or have turned back from following CHRIST. But there are still two or three who
stand firm. We believe that the people of Miaosheo
were greatly moved in a new way by the power of
GOD through the glorious death of his children."

————

John Stam's parting message—"may God be glorified whether by life or death" (Phil. 1:20)—written
in a letter after being taken captive, has been glo-
riously fulfilled.

1935   Today, fifty-three years after John and Betty met
their deaths by execution at the hands of the Communists, their name is still a byword for courage and
faith in the face of adversity. Helen is living in this
country with her husband and family, but does not
wish her identity and whereabouts to be made
known. The twentieth century up to its last decade
has been marked by the martyrdom of a great number
of Christians throughout the world. It would be in-
vidious to select one more than another for bravery
or commitment, yet no one would dispute John and
Betty Stam's supreme right to be included in the roll-
call of those whom the writer to the Hebrews de-
scribes as "of whom the world was not worthy" (Heb.
11:38) and the Book of Common Prayer, "the noble
army of martyrs."